FAT DOG THIN

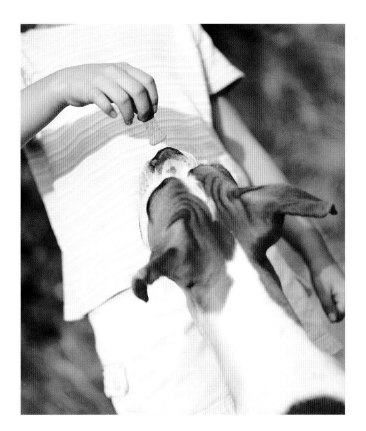

FAT DOG THIN

David Alderton

hamlyn

First published in Great Britain in 2007 by
Hamlyn, a division of Octopus Publishing Group Ltd
2–4 Heron Quays, London E14 4JP

Distributed in the United States and Canada by
Sterling Publishing Co., Inc.
387 Park Avenue South, New York, NY 10016-8810

ISBN-13: 978-0-600-61654-2
ISBN-10: 0-600-61654-1

A CIP catalogue record for this book is available from the British Library

Printed and bound in China

10 9 8 7 6 5 4 3 2 1

Picture Acknowledgements

Alamy 59, 99; /Digital Archive Japan 111; /Mark J. Barrett 132; /Juniors Bildarchiv 102, 115, 120; /Isobel Flynn 2 right, 94; /Andrew Linscott 97; /Mark Sherman 83; /Karen & Ian Stewart 133; /Bill Varie 7 left, 37; /Libby Welch 107; /Tony West 127; /willrolls.com 58.// **Ardea**/John Daniels 15, 76, 80; /Jean Michel Labat 90, 93, 96, 117, 121.// **Corbis UK Limited** 29; /Martin Harvey 65; /Gabe Palmer 84; /Paul A. Souders 51; /Dale C. Spartas 130.// **Doctor T. J. Dunn** 79 left, 79 right.// **Frank Lane Picture Agency**/Jim Brandenburg/Minden Pictures 11; /David Dalton 27; /Mitsuaki Iwago/Minden Pictures 34; /Mark Raycroft/Minden Pictures 26, 46, 95.// **Getty Images**/Dugald Bremner 126; /Peter Dazeley 25; /Kyle Newton 128; /Arne Pastoor 7 right, 139; /Steve Smith 12-13.// **Octopus Publishing Group Limited** 38, 40, 53, 73; /Anne Chambers 113; /Stephen Conroy 24; /Steve Gorton 17, 20; /Geoff Langan 9, 30, 39, 60, 119 top, 119 bottom, 122; /Angus Murray 45, 98; /A. Roslin-William 78.// **N.H.P.A.**/Susanne Danegger 63; /Yves Lanceau 36, 44, 55; /Ann & Steve Toon 136-137.// **Oxford Scientific Films**/Melanie Acevedo 86.// **Photodisc** 10.// **Photolibrary Group**/Hein van den Heuvel 6, 70; /Henry Horenstein 42; /Jim Corwin 62; /Lennette Newell 2 left, 109; /Southern Stock 103; /SuLu Images 135; /SW Production 23.

Contents

Introduction

page 6

1 The Root of the Problem

page 8

2 The Modern Day Dog

page 19

3 The Healthy Dog

page 32

4 Foods and Feeding

page 41

5 Exercising Your Dog

page 57

6 Lifestage Considerations

page 72

7 Planning for Fitness

page 89

8 Implementing the Plan

page 106

9 Preventing a Relapse

page 124

Ideal Weights by Breed

page 141

Index

page 143

Introduction

Dogs make wonderful companions and it is easy to find yourself compelled to feed them more than is necessary, giving them treats, tidbits and table scraps. While the occasional treat is harmless, a pet who is regularly overfed will quickly pile on the pounds. Similarly, a dog that is not getting enough exercise can develop a pattern of weight gain, becoming more lethargic and less inclined to run about. You might not even be aware of the problem at first, and it is often highlighted as a result of a veterinary visit.

By letting your dog get overweight, you are condemning your pet to an unnecessarily poor quality of life, and almost certainly, a shortened lifespan as well, but it is within the scope of every responsible owner to get their pet back in shape.

This book works to promote fitness and good health in your dog, with the ultimate view that prevention is better than cure. It also helps you break the cycle of weight gain and slim your dog down again if, for whatever reason, your pet has already become overweight. The first step towards correcting the problem is actually to face the fact

your pet is too heavy, so that you can then do something about the situation. If you are in any doubt, use the guide on page 16 to quickly assess your pet's condition.

Slimming your dog down is not a difficult process, but it does take time, so you cannot expect an instant slim-line pet. Do not despair, though, because help is at hand in the form of exercise ideas that will have you and your pet both living life to the full (see chapter 5). As well as giving him more exercise, you also need to restrict your dog's food intake, cutting back on the

number of calories which you are offering, so he burns off his unwanted body fat as explained in chapter 4.

You will have to be firm with yourself to cut out giving treats between meals. Not everyone finds this easy. If this applies to you, then consider the fact that your dog will ultimately live a longer, better quality of life if you stick to the guidelines here. By assessing your dog's condition, setting a realistic target, and sticking to the weight-loss plan, you will soon find your new routine becomes as much a part of your life as your much-loved pet.

The Root of the Problem

The lives of dogs have been inextricably linked with ours for at least 15,000 years, extending right back to the start of the domestication process. Their pattern of life has evolved throughout this period, shaped largely by the way human society has developed, and continues to do so. For much of this time, dogs have been working companions, carrying out a variety of tasks to fulfil human needs.

Over recent years, however, as technology has become increasingly important, so the role of dogs has altered significantly, and they are now kept mainly as household pets. Indeed, many tasks formerly undertaken by dogs, such as that of the so-called 'turnspit', a dog that used to work a treadmill that turned a roasting joint of meat over an open fire in the kitchen, have long been carried out by mechanical and technological means.

Our increasing reliance on technology goes some way to explaining why obesity has become a major problem in dogs today, but is a condition that was essentially unknown in their working ancestors. As our own daily lives have become more sedentary and obesity levels among people are rising, so it is not surprising that our closest companion has been similarly affected, with one in three dogs on average being considered not just overweight but clinically obese.

Ironically, as in the case of human medicine, advances in the veterinary field have now opened the way for dogs to live longer than ever before, but sadly the epidemic of obesity threatens to curtail the lives of many pets. At the very least, obesity is likely to have a highly detrimental impact upon a dog's quality of life, and create significant health problems. While people are rightly concerned about dogs that are neglected and starved by their owners, there is a general perception that allowing a dog to become seriously overweight is not a significant issue. This could not be farther from the truth – an obese dog is actually being harmed by misplaced kindness on the part of the owner.

Part of the problem is that weight gain in dogs can be quite insidious, and you may not even be aware of the fact that your dog is overweight until it becomes very serious, often being highlighted

at a veterinary check-up. It is therefore important to monitor your pet's weight regularly, right through from puppyhood, or as soon as you acquire it, so that you remain alert to this risk. The sooner that you identify the problem, the easier it will be to take effective action to solve it.

The good news is that with determination on your part, and the help of veterinary advice and/or the weight-loss clinics that are run at many veterinary surgeries today, it is definitely possible to reverse the effects of obesity and restore your pet's quality of life.

Taking care of your dog's weight is a way to improve your pet's well-being. Through a combination of diet and exercise, even obese dogs can soon be put back on the track to good health.

In the Beginning

In order to understand the scale of the problem, and also why some breeds are at a greater risk of becoming obese than others, it is important to delve into the dog's ancestry. All of today's domestic dogs, including more than 350 different breeds, have evolved from a single species, in the guise of the Grey Wolf, whose distribution used to extend across most of the northern hemisphere.

Although there is still disagreement about when the domestication process began, it is unlikely that it occurred in a single locality at one particular time. Instead, various ancient human tribes probably kept wolf cubs that grew up with them, scavenging on human food, and then, if food was scarce, the wolves themselves were killed and eaten. This means that there were probably many false steps on the path to domestication. Gradually, however, in the case of those wolves that were able to survive and breed in these circumstances, their cubs formed a stronger association with humans, and it soon proved possible to train these emerging proto-dogs. The likelihood is that, at this stage, their value to humans grew significantly because they could then help to hunt down prey that might otherwise elude the human hunter.

The dog's senses are in many ways superior to ours. They have more acute hearing and can see more effectively in the dark, as well as being able to run faster. It is no surprise, therefore, that the oldest breed group – the hounds – were initially bred for hunting purposes. Depictions of sighthounds can be found in cave art in Africa dating back thousands of years – even before portrayals of such dogs in the culture of ancient Egypt – that bear an unmistakable similarity to the Greyhounds of today. They depended on their speed and athleticism to catch quarry, just like the wolf itself.

The Grey Wolf has evolved specialized survival instincts that are present to some extent in the domestic dog.

The Importance of Fitness

Life within a wolf pack is harsh, with fitness being a major determinant of whether a wolf lives or faces early death from starvation. While wolves will take advantage when food is plentiful, their overall level of activity means that they will not suffer from obesity. Nor does the size of the prey affect a wolf's susceptibility to obesity, but instead influences the size of the pack. In northern Canada, for example, where large Moose are commonly hunted, a pack of wolves may be comprised of as many as a dozen individuals, who use their collective energy to obtain food and share it around (though not always fairly); in the Arabian peninsula, where rodents and similar small prey tend to form the basis of a wolf's diet, wolves are more likely to be encountered in pairs, or even individually. Each adult wolf typically requires 2.5–6 kg (5½–13 lb) of food per day, although there may be days when prey is scarce, and so wolves are forced to scavenge, eating carcasses and even vegetable matter, if they are not to starve.

The adaptability of wolves, which is manifest in the domestic dog, is still apparent today, even in areas where the species has been hunted to the verge of extinction. The few surviving grey wolves in Italy may be drawn to scavenge on landfill rubbish dumps, where they come into contact

Wolves hunt in packs as well as alone, depending on the area that they inhabit and the availability of food, which can change throughout the year.

with stray dogs and can mate with them, creating wolf-dog hybrids.

This instinct to scavenge is very strong in domestic dogs, and is one of the characteristics that can predispose them to obesity. They will frequently act in this way whenever they have the opportunity, from ripping apart bin bags containing discarded food outdoors to stealing groceries left within their reach in the home. Such behaviour is not a reflection of whether they are hungry or not, but rather it indicates a desire to take advantage of additional food when it is available in case of a shortage later.

Working Tasks

As human communities started to become more settled, so different types of dog breeds developed. Some breeds became bigger, which meant that they increased not just in size but also in weight, and had bigger appetites. They were valued as guardians of property, and some, such as the fearsome Bandogs, were even used in battle.

In the far north, dogs were a vital means of transport, pulling sleds, and they are still used for this purpose in some areas. This group of dogs bears the closest resemblance to wolves in terms of appearance. Described as the Spitz breeds, they have a head shape and raised ears that clearly display their lupine origins. Their dense fur gives good protection against the cold, while their high calorie requirements have been traditionally met from a high-fat diet provided by the blubber of marine mammals such as seals. Scenthounds emerged at a later stage than sighthounds, hunting in wooded country that demanded a different technique. Whereas sighthounds relied on their blistering pace and acute vision to outpace quarry, scenthounds utilized their keen sense of smell and stamina to track down their target, working in packs.

Other breeds were also developed as part of the hunting tradition. Pointers and spaniels have a long history, being particularly valued for their skill in finding and indicating the presence of quarry. Retrievers, however, are of more recent origins, being developed for sport shooting in the early 1800s. In the field, they are bred to display

considerable stamina, locating birds that have been shot over land or entering water readily and swimming if necessary to retrieve fallen waterfowl.

Once agriculture became more widespread, other dogs were bred to herd and protect farmstock from potential predators such as wolves. While smaller breeds such as the Puli would work with the stock, other larger, fiercer dogs such as the Bergamasco were kept to deter attacks by wolves. Terrier breeds, whose origins lie mainly in Scotland and northern England, were

also originally kept on farms, being valued for controlling vermin (particularly rats). They confirm that size is no clear indicator of a dog's level of activity, as terriers are lively and feisty by nature.

The only group of dogs bred to have a naturally sedentary lifestyle were the companion breeds, often described as 'toys' because of their size. They have a surprisingly long history, extending back to ancient Roman times in Europe, and probably even earlier in Asia – Pekingese were so highly prized in China that to steal one of these dogs from the emperor was punishable by death. Small companion dogs were highly fashionable in the royal courts of Europe from the 1500s onwards, both as breeds in their own right and as what were effectively scaled-down miniatures of bigger breeds.

Sheepdogs expend lots of energy, both burning fuel through muscle use and also keeping mentally alert to their job, listening for commands from the owner.

Obesity Risks

The obesity equation is simple: a dog will put on weight if its food intake exceeds its energy needs, for growth, pregnancy or general activity. Most dog breeds were developed for working purposes rather than as lap dogs. Today, when given far less opportunity to exercise, combined with a plentiful supply of food, these breeds are most likely to put on weight. The overall larger size of these working breeds also means that they need fewer calories per kilogram or pound of body weight than their smaller relatives, because larger dogs need to expend less energy than smaller dogs to maintain their body temperature. As a result, larger dogs are actually more predisposed to becoming obese when overfed.

Feeding habits imprinted over centuries also play a part, with both Beagles and Basset Hounds (the scenthounds most widely kept as pets) being vulnerable to obesity, thanks to their innate gluttony – living communally in packs in kennels,

it was important for these dogs to feed readily, when food was available, or run the risk of being left hungry. In marked contrast, sighthounds such as the Greyhound and Whippet are far less susceptible to putting on weight. They do not display the same strong feeding instincts as scenthounds, being generally unlikely to eat in excess of their requirements, to the extent that they may often even leave surplus food in their bowl. This may be linked in part with the narrow-chested shape of their bodies, compared with the much broader stature of the Beagle, for example. The metabolism of sighthounds can also be significant: their fast pace places very different physiological demands on their bodies, compared with the slower speed and greater stamina that characterizes other working dogs. There is also no doubt that some breeds, including Beagles, seem more genetically disposed towards obesity than others.

BREEDS AT PARTICULAR RISK OF OBESITY

- **Basset Hound**
- **Beagle**
- **Cairn Terrier**
- **Cavalier King Charles Spaniel**
- **Dachshund**
- **Labrador Retriever**
- **Norwegian Elkhound**
- **Pug**
- **Rough Collie**
- **Shetland Sheepdog**

HOW TO WEIGH YOUR DOG

The simplest method of weighing your pet is to use the bathroom scales. It may be possible to persuade your dog to sit on the scales; if not, try standing on the scales holding your dog (depending on the size of your pet); then subtract your weight from the total. Be sure to write down your dog's weight in a diary so that you can keep a check on its progress. Always weigh your dog first thing in the morning if possible, rather than after a meal, to give an accurate and consistent figure. This will allow you to track your pet's weight to detect any unwanted upward trend, so you can take action before it becomes a significant problem.

The table on page 141 shows ideal weights for the commonest pure-bred dogs, as based on the guidelines provided by the breeders themselves.

For mongrels and cross-breeds you will need to refer to your vet as well as using the guide on the following page to determine whether your pet is the ideal weight, or is overweight. Beware in extreme cases of obesity you will find it hard to weigh the dog yourself as you will probably find it hard to lift your pet up.

How to Recognize an Obese Dog

Dogs are considered to be clinically obese when their body weight exceeds their ideal weight by 15 per cent or more. This may not seem a large amount. In the case of a Labrador Retriever, for example, whose weight should ideally not exceed 35 kg (75 lb), any that tip the scales over 39kg (86 lb) are considered to be obese. In the case of pure-bred dogs, it is easy to assess whether they are obese because their ideal weight is included as part of the breed standard under which dogs are judged at shows. In some of the largest

This Rough Collie is an ideal weight: hindquarters are lean and there is a definite narrowing at the waist. Even so, the long fur makes it hard to see clearly.

ASSESSING YOUR DOG'S WEIGHT

Target weight

- The ribs can be felt without difficulty under the coat, and there is a narrowing behind the ribs (this is the dog's waist).
- The top of the hip bones at the base of the tail can be felt.
- The abdomen feels taut.

Overweight

- The ribs are less discernible, with an increased amount of fat covering and the waist having largely disappeared.
- The hip bones are still discernible, but well-covered by fat.
- The abdomen is starting to appear paunchy.

Obese

- It is now impossible to feel the dog's ribs, thanks to the covering of fat, while the abdomen has ballooned out, obscuring the waist.
- The top of the hip bones are now obscured by fat.
- The abdomen is likely to be hanging down, creating a paunch.

breeds, there may be some slight variance in weight between the sexes, with male dogs tending to attain a larger size and therefore weighing correspondingly more as a result.

In the case of non-pedigree dogs, where there are no prescribed weights, you should assess their body condition in order to gain a clear insight into their ideal weight, whether they are mongrels or cross-breds resulting from the mating of two or more different breeds. The ribs provide one of the most obvious and valuable indicators of a dog's condition (see box on page 16).

Beware if your dog is long-coated because its coat can mask a gain in weight. This is why, aside from weighing your dog regularly, you should also check its physical condition during grooming. It is much easier to monitor breeds such as Whippets that have very short coats, simply by their appearance, although you should still weigh your dog to be certain of its weight.

DOG BREEDS AND THEIR ORIGINAL PURPOSES

Gundogs
These industrious dogs were bred as shooting companions, firstly indicating the presence of game and then retrieving it, which sometimes entailed swimming. (e.g. Labrador, Retriever)

Hounds
Active and athletic by nature, bred to hunt a wide variety of quarry, from rabbits to wild boar, by scent or by sight, depending on the particular breed. (e.g. Beagle, Irish Wolfhound)

Pastoral
Used to working with livestock, these dogs are intelligent, responsive and active by nature. They can easily become bored if confined in the home for long periods. (e.g. German Shepherd Dog, Old English Sheepdog)

Terriers
Terriers are feisty dogs that traditionally hunted rodents on farms, as well as driving foxes out of their burrows. Tough and hardy, some breeds were formerly used for fighting. (e.g. West Highland White Terrier)

Toys
Small dogs developed as companions, sometimes being scaled-down versions of larger breeds. Can have mobility problems, especially if they are overweight. (e.g. Chihuahua, Pug)

Utility
These working dogs were bred to undertake a wide variety of tasks, from pulling carts to acting as guardians. Often quite large and strong. (e.g. Chow Chow, Dalmatian)

The Modern Day Dog

For working dogs, the switch from a life of activity to that of a fireside companion is a recent development, beginning just over a century ago. This is actually a very short period of time in the context of the overall domestication process of the dog. The shift towards dogs becoming sought-after household pets rather than working companions was a reflection of the major changes that were taking place in society in the 19th century. It occurred largely as a result of the rising affluence and influence of the middle classes in Europe and the United States, and was driven by the Victorian pursuit of 'fancying' – the selective breeding of both plants and animals for pleasure – and the rise of interest in competitive shows. Judging standards were soon established, and the appearance of breeds became more clearly defined as a result, with breeders striving to create dogs that corresponded as closely as possible to the perceived ideal. How a dog compares to the ideal breed standard, rather than how it compares to the other dogs in the class, is still the yardstick used for judging purposes.

An Englishman called Charles Cruft founded the world-famous dog show that now bears his name. His first major event, held in 1891 in London, was a huge success, drawing together a wide range of breeds for the first time and even attracting support from Queen Victoria, who was a devoted dog lover. Across the Atlantic, the American Kennel Club was founded in 1883, followed by its Canadian counterpart a year later, and soon similar events such as the Westminster Dog Show were also drawing large numbers of visitors, keen both to see and acquire dogs as pets.

Basset Hounds are prone to weight gain, due to their innate gluttony as well as their need for long bouts of relatively gentle exercise. They love to sniff things when they go out rather than run around for long periods.

Changing Perceptions

The popularity of dog shows quickly led to a blurring of the widely differing origins of the various breeds. The breeds were assessed purely in aesthetic terms, with relatively little consideration being given to their backgrounds. Previously only toy breeds had been kept as companions, but it soon seemed that any breed could fulfil this role.

People today tend to choose a breed of dog as a pet largely, if not exclusively, on the basis of its appearance, rather than delving into its ancestry and discovering more about its original purpose. Many breeds, of course, are descended from active, working stock. Kept in the home for much of the day, with relatively little opportunity to exercise and provided with plenty of food, it is not surprising that these dogs are now at much greater risk of becoming obese, compared with their working ancestors.

Just as our lives have become less physically demanding in many cases, the same applies to dogs, and this has left both us and our pets vulnerable to obesity. Perhaps not surprisingly, various studies have revealed that there is a clear link between the fitness and obesity levels of dogs and those of their owners.

The Rise of the Dog Food Industry

Another significant factor that underpinned Cruft's enthusiasm for dog shows has also had a major impact on the way that dogs are now kept. A few years before Cruft's first dog show, an entrepreneur called James Spratt had seen the potential for a new market, buying up uneaten biscuits from ships arriving in the docks. He employed Cruft and other representatives to visit the great estates of the period, offering these stale biscuits for sale as dog food, to be used in the kennels. Up until this stage, dogs had been fed on various diets, with no prepared food being available.

However, once a market began to emerge for dog food, this then led to interest in creating specific foods to meet different dogs' needs. By simplifying the feeding process in this way, it became much easier for people to care for dogs, and this helped to increase their popularity as pets. The massive pet food industry of today has grown up in parallel with the dog show scene, just as Spratt and Cruft envisaged. This has helped to encourage dog ownership, and brought significant benefits both for owners and pets. Owners no longer have to provide food such as raw tripe for their dogs, with scientific studies having led to a much greater understanding of dogs' nutritional needs, which is reflected in the advanced formulations of foods available for them today.

Modern Dog Food Developments

Increasing specialization and niche marketing over recent years has led to the creation not just of foods for particular groups, such as working dogs, but also to an expanding range of diets specifically formulated for individual breeds, extending from German Shepherd dogs to Bulldogs. There are also lifestage diets, catering for dogs of different ages from puppyhood through to old age, as well as slimming diets.

The convenience factor associated with complete dog foods, whether you are using canned or pouched food, a semi-moist food or a dry diet, has made it much easier to care for dogs than when feeding a fresh food diet. Pets can now be fed with minimum preparation, because you know that these prepared foods have been formulated to contain everything necessary to meet the dog's nutritional requirements.

The Cost of Convenience

The ease of convenience foods underlies, at least in part, the rising levels of obesity seen in the dog population today. Sales of canned food have declined significantly over the past decade, with dry foods becoming the pre-eminent choice in the marketplace. In contrast, semi-moist foods that were intended to offer the palatability of canned food, but with greater longevity, have never really become popular.

The switch to dry food occurred because canned food is less convenient. The latter is relatively heavy to carry, bulky to store and, once opened, it deteriorates rapidly in warm weather if not eaten up. It smells strongly and can also attract flies as well. Dry food is now in the ascendancy, with packs typically containing enough food to last a dog perhaps two weeks or more. It provides a concentrated source of energy, and will not deteriorate rapidly like canned food, because its water content is much lower.

Although people tend to provide their dog with no more than is necessary when using canned food, because a can only contains one or two meals, it is easy to pour a large portion of dry food into a dog's bowl, perhaps topping it up regularly without thinking about the quantity. It is therefore much easier to overfeed a dog unintentionally with dry food. Even if you only offer a small amount in excess of the recommendation on the pack, this increase in calories will soon mount up if you do so on a regular basis. See page 46 for calorie comparisons between the different food.

Food – especially dry food – must be measured out carefully to prevent insidious weight gain. Teach younger family members how to measure out the food, or they may overfeed the dog inadvertently.

Treats

Calories can quickly mount up, particularly when treats are used as rewards during training. One way to limit this is to break the treats into tiny pieces rather than giving them whole.

Another area of the dog food industry that has grown dramatically over recent years is that of 'treats'. Used occasionally, these should not have any harmful effect on a dog's weight, but do not encourage a situation where your pet comes to expect treats. This can easily happen if you use treats as rewards while training a puppy. This is simply not necessary, and the regular use of treats may easily contribute to your dog becoming overweight at a young age.

Praising your dog with a positive tone of voice is often more effective as a way of encouraging it to respond to your commands as required, because this causes the dog to focus on you rather that on treats that distract from the training routine. There are also healthy low-calorie alternatives that can be used as treats, such as pieces of carrot or a slice of dessert apple.

MEASURING FOOD

Always read the feeding instructions carefully on dog food. Measure out the amount your dog needs with a clean plastic container and kitchen scales. Mark the level on the container and use it as a scoop in the future for dry food to prevent over-feeding. Remember if you switch to another formulation or brand of food, the feeding recommendations may differ.

Overindulgence

Owners sometimes unconsciously contribute to their dog's weight problems by overindulging their pets. An interesting study carried out in Germany compared the actions of owners who had obese dogs with those whose dogs were at their optimal weight. The researchers discovered that table scraps were fed more often to dogs that were obese, and their owners used food much more as a way of communicating with their pets, feeding them on demand.

It also emerged that these owners were mirroring their own requirements in a way, because they also tended to be obese, compared with the dogs and owners in the other group. Generally, owners whose dogs were obese were also less aware of the precise nutritional needs of their pets, and responded to attention from their pets by giving tidbits, when a more appropriate course of action might have been to take the dog out for a walk or play with their pet, providing exercise.

Dogs, like humans, are creatures of habit, and they can quickly come to expect treats if they are offered as rewards for good behaviour. You must limit these or your dog will be at risk of becoming overweight.

Get in Shape with the Help of Your Dog

If you yourself are overweight, there is no reason why you cannot get back into shape with the help of your pet – benefiting you both. A recent trial carried out in the United States over the course of a year by a major pet food manufacturer and the Northwestern Memorial Hospital in Illinois produced some interesting findings. Involving owners and dogs who were both overweight, the participants were divided into three groups: dogs on their own; people alone; and dogs and people together.

Where owners were engaged in a fitness programme alongside their pets, they were more likely to complete the programme, compared with the scenario of the dog being slimmed down on its own by the owner. The majority of the additional exercise that took place entailed the owner working out alongside the pet, so both owner and dog ended up in better shape. Over the course of the year, dogs taking part lost up to 16 kg (35 lb), while the best result achieved by an owner was a loss of 23 kg (51 lb). Essentially, a dog needs a similar minimum amount of aerobic exercise to ourselves, averaging out at a minimum of half an hour or so daily.

It has also been known for some time that dog owners who suffer heart attacks have a significantly better survival rate compared to those recovering from heart attacks without dogs. This is likely to be due, at least in part, to the fact the former are taking regular exercise with their pets.

Exercising with your dog will help both you and your pet to lose weight and get in shape, as well as strengthening the bond between you.

Other Reasons for Canine Obesity

Aside from food intake and exercise needs, there are two other factors that can be cited in the rising levels of obesity among dogs. The first is that more pets are now being neutered than in the past. This brings a number of significant benefits, such as reducing the likelihood of male dogs straying, as well as, most obviously, unwanted litters of puppies – quite apart from avoiding the serious medical complications that can sometimes arise during pregnancy in elderly bitches.

However, this surgery also impacts on the dog's metabolism to the extent that its food intake must be significantly reduced after surgery, possibly by as much as 30 per cent, to prevent associated unwanted gain in weight. If you do not readjust your dog's food intake after neutering, it will inevitably start to put on weight, even if the amount of exercise that your pet is having does not change. Unfortunately, this factor is often overlooked, particularly in the feeding instructions on dog food, so many owners are unaware of this potential problem.

The other factor that has led to an increase in the overall level of obesity in the canine population is simply the fact that dogs are now living longer than at any stage in the past. However, their nutritional needs change with age, which is why it is important to adjust the food intake of older dogs and to reduce the number of calories that they are eating. Otherwise, as your dog's level of activity naturally declines with age, its excess food intake will be reflected in an expanding waistline and other associated signs of obesity. It can be particularly difficult to slim down an older dog, simply because, by this stage in life, dogs are naturally less active and may also be suffering from various conditions that may restrict their ability to exercise. (See chapter 6 for more information on illness-related obesity and the effects of old age.)

Dogs lose muscle mass in old age and become less active, so they will put on weight if their food intake is not reduced to reflect their changing lifestyle.

Lifestyle Changes

Another, less apparent, reason why pets today are becoming increasingly overweight is that our own lifestyles are changing. During a dog's lifetime, an owner's life is likely to change in various ways. Increased work or relationship demands, for example, can mean that you have less time available to attend to your pet's needs. The usual daily walks are at times curtailed, and you may not have as much time to play with your pet at home. The dog is left alone for longer, and does not have as much opportunity to stay active. In these situations, if the dog still eats the same amount, but is taking less exercise, it is likely to gain weight over a period of time.

Another consequence of neglecting your pet is that your dog is likely to become bored and may start to be less responsive to you as a result.

In order to pacify your pet, you may then rely more heavily on treats, which will again affect your pet's expanding waist-line. Boredom can also encourage your dog to attempt to steal food, and so create additional weight problems. If you think that you are likely to be late home in the evening, do not be tempted to pour more food into your dog's bowl before you go out. This is not necessary, and will be counter-productive, simply serving to encourage your pet to eat more than is required.

Boredom can be a key contributing factor to canine obesity. A dog will overeat out of boredom if food is available, and may become lethargic. The best cure for lethargy, of course, is regular exercise.

THE REAL BENEFITS OF WEIGHT LOSS

A dog that is a healthy weight will enjoy a much better quality of life than an obese dog. If you find yourself wavering in your commitment, it is worth reminding yourself of the real benefits of losing weight. The main benefits of controlling weight are:

- **Better health (which means lower veterinary bills for you)**
- **Improved fitness**
- **A longer lifespan**
- **Better chances of survival if surgery is ever required**
- **A more responsive companion for you.**

DOG-WALKING SERVICES

If you suffer an accident or ill-health that makes walking difficult, or you have to be away from home for longer periods each day, help with walking your dog is available in the form of dog-walking services. These services arrange for someone else to walk your dog regularly, thereby preventing your dog from putting on weight through lack of exercise or becoming bored at home. Check the dog walker's references first, and be certain that they are appropriately insured before entrusting them with the temporary care of your dog each day.

Meeting your dog's exercise needs is a key responsibility for all owners. If one day you cannot, arrange for someone else to take your pet for a walk.

Keep Feeding and Exercise Separate

One of the most important things in the battle against obesity is to encourage your dog to take more exercise. It is important, however, to keep feeding and exercise separate, particularly in the case of larger dogs, as well as those with narrow, deep chests, such as the Irish Wolfhound.

If you take your dog out for a run shortly after a meal, there is a risk that it could suffer from bloat, which is a life-threatening condition requiring emergency veterinary treatment. Here, the stomach becomes dilated by air as well as the food present, causing it to become grossly distended. It then twists on itself, this movement being described as 'volvulus'. Consequently, the food cannot pass out of the stomach into the small intestine because the exit is blocked, while the distortion of the stomach impacts on the positioning of other organs in the abdomen. External swelling of this area of the body will be evident, and the dog's condition will deteriorate rapidly as shock sets in. Even if you simply suspect that your dog may have stolen some food, wait a couple of hours before taking it out for a walk as a precautionary measure.

Unfortunately, once a dog has suffered from an episode of bloat, there is an increased possibility that it may recur in the future. Offering smaller meals is no guarantee of overcoming the problem, with the best preventative measure being to feed your dog after exercise not before.

WHY IS YOUR DOG PUTTING ON WEIGHT?

There are several reasons your dog may be putting on weight, including one or more of the following :
- You have less time to exercise your pet.
- Your dog's opportunity to run off the leash and to play have been reduced.
- You have changed the type of dog food.
- You are over-feeding your pet by giving table scraps and/or giving too many treats.
- Your dog is getting food elsewhere, perhaps stealing it from another pet in the home.
- Your dog is growing older and becoming naturally less active.

The Healthy Dog

Although dogs often appear to be gluttons, devouring whatever is placed in front of them, they do have favourite foods. Under normal circumstances, for example, a dog will instinctively eat meat rather than vegetable protein. Dogs generally prefer beef, followed by pork and lamb. However, this is not to suggest that they prefer red meat consistently over white meat, because they will usually feed on chicken in preference to horse meat. Individual dogs do differ in their tastes, though, and it is probable that a dog's feeding preferences develop at a very early stage in life, with food flavours passing across in the bitch's breast milk to her puppies. This is likely to condition the puppies to take solid food more readily once the weaning process starts, because they will then instinctively recognize the food as being edible.

Food Preferences

An experiment carried out with Chow Chow puppies many years ago attempted to discover what influenced their choice of food. The young dogs were divided into three groups and fed exclusively on different diets from weaning up to the age of six months (which is often regarded as the end of puppyhood). One group was reared entirely on mixed vegetarian foods, while another was kept on a soya bean diet, and the third was fed on a varied diet including meat.

It was found that the puppies receiving the soya bean food would eat nothing else, whereas those that had been reared on vegetables would not feed on meat. The puppies in the third group, which had been provided with a much greater variety of choices, would readily take other foods, except those that were sour, stale or bitter – all of which could be suggestive of inedible and potentially harmful items. This shows that it is indeed possible to influence the life-long feeding preferences of puppies, and even deter them from sampling other types of food later in life.

Other less drastic experiments have found that, when puppies of small breeds, such as Yorkshire Terriers and Dachshunds, have been kept exclusively on a particular type of puppy food up until the age of two years, rather than being switched to a standard food at about six months,

DIFFERENT TYPES OF FOOD

WET	SEMI-MOIST	DRY	FROZEN MEAT	HOME-COOKED
Has a high moisture content and is typically sold in cans. Individual servings are sold in pouches and foil trays.	High in salt and resembling meat in texture. Sold in sachets it dries out once opened. Contains sugar, and is unsuitable for diabetic dogs.	A concentrated source of energy, it often is sold in bags of various sizes, does not require refrigeration, but must be kept away from light.	This needs to be defrosted and cooked. You may also need to add biscuit to it before feeding. Not necessarily a balanced diet.	You control the ingredients in your dog's food, but it can be hard to devise a balanced diet or judge the amount of food needed.

Cavalier King Charles Spaniels are prone to obesity,
so take care not to overfeed them and make sure
that you monitor their weight from puppyhood.

they are far less inclined to sample new foods compared with puppies that have been given a range of different foods through this period.

This early development of food preferences makes it clear that the roots of obesity can often be traced back to the formative stages of a dog's life. A young dog that receives a highly calorific puppy food for longer than recommended by the manufacturer, for example, may be less inclined to eat a lower-calorie ration in due course, increasing the risk that it will become overweight as it grows older. When an owner first introduces the new lower-calorie food to the dog, they may find that the dog largely ignores the food. Many owners will not purchase the new food again, reverting to their original food, even though this may not reflect the dog's changing nutritional needs. A vicious cycle is therefore being created which can develop into a feeding problem.

Even if you take advantage of the nutritional benefits of using a puppy food at this early stage in your pet's upbringing, always try to persuade a puppy to sample a range of different foods to encourage it to be less fussy about its food later in life. You will then be able to adjust your dog's diet more easily when you need to in the future, switching to a standard, senior or even a weight-loss ration.

FOOD TEXTURE

The texture of food has been shown to greatly influence its palatability, with dogs generally preferring fresh and wet food over semi-moist and dry food if given a free choice. Do not be surprised if your dog becomes less inclined to eat a particular brand of food after being sick. The memory of the illness becomes linked with the food, although this phase will pass.

Dog breeds that have been identified as being most susceptible to obesity, such as the Labrador Retriever and the Cavalier King Charles Spaniel, have been shown to be the least fussy about their food. These breeds readily eat lots of different foods, and can be persuaded to switch diets very easily. On the other hand, some small breeds such as Chihuahuas can be very particular about what they eat, often as the result of being conditioned by their owner's responses. A dog that rejects dry food to find this is then replaced by a more tasty wet food option, for example, will learn to carry on behaving in this way to gain his dish of choice.

Chihuahuas are notoriously fussy eaters, so feeding them a varied diet from an early age will help prevent them from developing awkward food preferences.

The Importance of Variety

A potential effect of feeding dogs on a prepared food is that they may receive little variety in their diet. In the wild, wolves will take a number of different prey species through the year. By varying your pet's diet, you will encourage your dog to become more interested in its food, and this may encourage greater activity as well. By offering different types of food, you should notice that your dog becomes more lively and alert when being fed, paying greater attention to what is in the food bowl. Dogs tend to sleep for quite long periods each day anyway, and if always fed on the same food and given a standard exercise routine, they can become rather bored.

Predators such as the Grey Wolf have evolved alert, problem-solving brains that are essential for their survival. They literally need to out think their prey in order to ensure their own survival. Domestic dogs need challenges in their lives, but try to ensure that meal times are fixed, or you are likely to find that your pet becomes restless. Dogs do appreciate a basic routine, with set feeding and exercise times, but variety within these areas will help to keep your pet alert and contribute to your dog's mental and physical fitness.

One of the easiest ways to provide variety is to use a combination of canned and dry food. These foods can be offered alternately, and you can obviously choose different flavours as well. The most important thing, whatever type of food you are using, is to be sure that you know how many calories you are giving your pet. Do not be tempted to add small additional amounts of food in the form of table scraps to your dog's regular diet to provide variety, because you will probably find that your pet starts to put on weight. It is also important to make dietary changes gradually, in order to minimize the risk of digestive upsets.

Having set meal-times instils in a dog that food will not come on demand and begging for it at any other time of the day will not result in extra food.

The Dangers of Puppy Fat

Studies into the causes of obesity are starting to reveal some remarkable findings. The seeds of the obesity problem in later life can be traced right back to early puppyhood. Young dogs at this stage do have fat cells in their bodies, and a degree of fat is in fact beneficial. Subcutaneous fat located below the skin helps to insulate the body, preventing heat loss, which can be a particular problem faced by puppies and small dogs. This is partly because their body mass relative to their surface area is quite small and, as a result, they can lose heat rapidly from their bodies. Puppies are also not able to control their own body temperature effectively early in life, with the litter huddling together to keep warm.

Dogs of all breeds are of a similar size at birth, and only as they grow do discrepancies in size become apparent – ranging from the tiny Chihuahua that measures about 15 cm (6 in) to the top of the shoulder, up to an Irish Wolfhound that may stand over 90cm (36 in) tall. Early feeding habits are obviously critical, both for the bitch during the period that the puppies are suckling and then in the post-weaning period for the young dogs themselves.

If puppies become too fat at this early stage, their bodies start to produce many more fat cells than normal. This is why young dogs that become overweight early in life are far more likely to be obese when they are older. However, the situation is significantly different in the case of an older dog that becomes fat, because it is no longer growing and therefore has fewer fat cells in its body; as a result, it can be slimmed down more easily.

A Golden Retriever puppy, while a similar size at birth to a Jack Russell Terrier, will overtake the smaller breed in size and stature in a matter of weeks.

Training: Go Easy on Treats

If you allow a young dog to become fat, you are leaving your pet exposed to a greater risk of obesity throughout its life. When you acquire a puppy, be sure that you know what its target weight should be as an adult dog and monitor its progress. In the case of mongrels and cross-bred puppies, where it is difficult to gauge a target weight, it is especially important to check their physical condition regularly (see page 16). In the early stages it is very easy to spoil a puppy with treats, especially once training starts. However, there is no need to rely heavily on treats as part of the training process, and your dog will not miss treats if you do not provide them.

Plenty of encouragement is usually adequate by way of a reward when the puppy responds as required. If you start giving treats, your dog will soon come to expect them, with the result that you yourself will become conditioned to provide treats for your pet. This creates a cycle of dependency that can prove hard to break.

Your dog will respond by expecting a treat when it performs a particular behaviour, and this can actually create problems in the training programme. You may well find that it becomes difficult to persuade your pet to move on to a new element of the training without providing the anticipated treat. If you only occasionally give a treat, by way of encouragement, this is likely to maintain your pet's concentration more effectively, simply because the dog is aware that it may be rewarded with a treat if it behaves as required, but this is not a certainty.

CLICKERS

The use of clickers for training dogs has become very popular in recent years, with the sound of the clicker serving to indicate to the dog that it has responded as required. This reinforces the newly learned behaviour in the dog's mind.

It is important that you do not give your dog a treat every time that you click, as an associated reward, because this will soon lead to an expanding waistline. Use alternatives to treats, such as praising your pet when it responds appropriately. If you do occasionally want to provide food treats, avoid calorie-laden options, replacing them with healthier choices such as a small piece of carrot or dessert apple.

The Danger of Bribes

Do not allow yourself to be forced into a situation with your dog where you need to bribe it with food to behave properly. This is no substitute for proper training. First and foremost, you need to be sure that your dog will react in accordance with your instructions, rather than simply in response to a treat. It might even make the difference between life and death for your pet, because if your dog is out of control and runs into the street, it could easily end up being fatally injured by a vehicle. On the other hand, a well-trained dog should stay when told to do so, irrespective of whether or not a treat is being given for reacting in this way.

Indeed, in some cases, there is no doubt that using treats as bribes can actually be

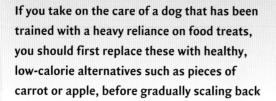

Apple slices can be a substitute for unhealthy treats, although not dried ones which can bloat the stomach if too many are eaten.

counter-productive. You may well find that your dog starts behaving badly, taking advantage of the situation in the certain knowledge that you will bribe it to behave differently. The situation will be even worse if you are using commercial treats, rather than pieces of fruit or vegetable, because these are laden with calories. Inevitably, piled on top of the dog's regular meals, and given several times every day, treats of this type will cause significant weight gain. They will result in your pet becoming obese before too long, unless you take steps to address the situation.

BREAKING THE BRIBERY CYCLE

If you take on the care of a dog that has been trained with a heavy reliance on food treats, you should first replace these with healthy, low-calorie alternatives such as pieces of carrot or apple, before gradually scaling back the frequency of giving the rewards. This will increase your pet's responsiveness, being no longer sure that a treat will be given, ultimately breaking the dog's dependence on treats as part of the training process.

Foods and Feeding

To prevent your dog from putting on unwanted weight, it is important to match food intake to energy requirements. If the calorific content of the food exceeds the calories that a dog needs for its level of activity, the dog's weight will start to increase accordingly. If this happens, you need to tilt the balance the other way, ensuring that, by a gradual reduction in the calorific value of its diet, the dog's fat stores are utilized, leading to weight loss.

Remember that dogs can have appetites far in excess of their calorific needs, so you cannot rely on a dog to show any restraint. Scent plays a key role in attracting a dog to food, and helping to determine what is edible. Dogs are gluttonous eaters, which is another characteristic inherited from their wolf ancestor. Their teeth are not adept at chewing food, but they are effective at tearing it apart, allowing them to swallow large chunks of meat.

How Dogs Eat

The conspicuous pointed canines at the front of a dog's mouth help to hold food, but they are blunted at their tips and are not especially sharp. It is actually the special carnassial teeth, located farther back in the mouth that allow the dog to slice through large chunks of food, cutting off pieces that can be swallowed easily. These carnassial teeth consist of the last premolar in the upper jaw and the first molar in the lower jaw, both of which are modified for this purpose. You can spot them quite easily when you open a dog's mouth or are cleaning its teeth, because the last premolar in each upper jaw is significantly larger than those in front of it. Also, the raised areas of these teeth, known as cusps, are not evident at the rear of this premolar or, indeed, the molar with which it overlaps in the lower jaw.

At the front of the carnassial teeth, the cusps are not aligned, so they do not slot into the corresponding gap in the tooth of the other jaw, which is a feature of the other teeth. This arrangement creates a scissor-like effect, making the carnassial teeth effective at slicing through flesh. When using its carnassial teeth, a dog has a characteristic pose, keeping its head relatively low and tilted to one side. The dog can swallow the piece of meat in its mouth, then slice through the next piece.

Dogs use the carnassial teeth towards the back of the mouth to slice off pieces of food to swallow.

Dog Foods and the Teeth

Dogs that are fed on prepared foods tend not to use their carnassial teeth, instead picking up the food with their incisor teeth at the front of the mouth. They will not chew it to any significant extent, tending simply to gulp it down. This can be an advantage with a dry diet. Deposits of plaque can build up at the base of the teeth adjacent to the gum line. These can harden into tartar and cause inflammation that, if unchecked, will lead to erosion of the gum line. This in turn will weaken the anchorage of the tooth in the jaws, as well as allow bacteria to reach the root and create a painful abscess. Dry food has an advantage over wet food in that it does not adhere as easily to the teeth, thereby reducing the risk of tartar. In addition, the slightly abrasive nature of dry food helps to prevent the build-up of plaque when a dog does chew its food. Whatever food you use, brushing your dog's teeth regularly using a special canine toothpaste and brush will minimize the problem. Any significant build-up of tartar on the teeth is likely to cause halitosis (bad breath).

The Digestive Process

Dogs gulp down their food simply because, in a pack situation, there may not be enough for every pack member to eat its fill. There is also the risk in the wild that other, larger species may move in on the kill, displacing them. Once the food has passed from the stomach into the small intestine, the digestion process starts. A variety of enzymes break down the food into its core chemical constituents, which are then absorbed through the wall of the small intestine and into the blood stream. Carbohydrate is especially important in regulating a dog's appetite; this is absorbed as glucose, with the glucose content of the blood registering on the part of the brain known as the hypothalamus. When the blood sugar rises to a certain level, the dog's appetite declines and it will stop eating for a period. It is therefore possible to affect a dog's appetite by providing different types of carbohydrate that are broken down into glucose at varying rates.

If you are seeking to reduce your dog's weight, it is obviously useful to curb its appetite, and this can be achieved partly by modifying the carbohydrate source in its diet. This is especially significant if you are preparing the dog's food yourself, rather than using a prepared diet. Using barley as a source of carbohydrate rather than rice is preferable here, because the absorption rate of the sugar into the body is slower with barley than rice, so prevents a sudden peak followed by a rapid fall-off in the circulation. Do not overload your dog's carbohydrate intake in an attempt to curb its appetite, though, because the excess will be converted and stored in the body as fat.

Vegetarianism

The natural diet of the dog's ancestor, the Grey Wolf, is meat-based rather than consisting of cereals, as reflected by its dental pattern (although many wild canids eat fruit and berries occasionally). Even so, it is possible to maintain dogs satisfactorily on vegetarian diets, and there are various prepared foods of this type available. There is no evidence that dogs will be more at risk of becoming obese on this type of food, compared with a more standard meat-based diet.

Because the protein content of this type of dog food is of vegetable origin rather than derived

from meat, it is important to ensure that your pet is not at risk of developing an essential amino acid deficiency. Amino acids are the building blocks of protein. Some of these cannot be manufactured in the body, so they have to be present in the dog's diet to prevent a deficiency from arising. However, if you use a formulated vegetarian food rather than preparing the diet yourself, this should not be a worry because the food will have been supplemented accordingly.

The high fibre content of some vegetarian diets may actually be beneficial in helping a dog to lose weight, because the fibre serves to bulk up the dog's ration without being full of calories. However, there may be difficulties if you also have a cat in your household, because it is not possible to maintain cats in good health on a vegetarian diet. You may find that your dog resorts to stealing your cat's meat-based food, which will have a higher protein content and be more palatable than the dog's own diet, in addition to eating its own vegetarian food. It is therefore always a good idea to ensure that your cat's food is out of reach of your dog, because the temptation to eat the cat's food will be too great; you will find this is the case whether or not you are feeding your dog a vegetarian diet. The result could be an increase in your dog's weight – and a hungry cat.

Basset Hounds are at particular risk of obesity, and will always eat if food is available. Some have been known to have unusual tastes, including fruit.

Input Versus Output

Various factors influence the quantity of food that your dog needs, the most significant being its age. Puppies are growing and active by nature, so they require significantly more calories than middle-aged dogs. When a dog becomes older, its calorific requirements fall as the result of its declining level of activity. It is therefore important to adjust the amount of calories that you are providing, to meet your pet's changing needs. A dog will inevitably gain weight as it becomes older; many owners fail to appreciate this, which partly explains why older dogs are most likely to be obese. Thankfully, this is something that pet food manufacturers have sought to address through the introduction of so-called 'lifestage' diets, catering for dogs of different ages.

The size of the dog also has a significant impact on its calorific requirement. Larger dogs have a lower calorific requirement per kilogram or pound of body weight compared with small toy dogs. This may be explained in part by their greater bulk, in that they need to expend proportionately less energy maintaining their body temperature. As larger breeds also have a shorter life expectancy than their smaller cousins, they should be switched to a senior ration at a slightly earlier stage. There is actually no precise definition of when a dog becomes a senior, but it is generally from the age of eight years onwards. Larger breeds can be transferred to a senior diet a year or so earlier because they may only live for 10 years or so, whereas smaller breeds are likely to live into their teens. There are a number of differences between a senior diet and an ordinary ration, but one of the most significant is the reduction in the calorific content, which helps to prevent obesity.

As with a human diet, a balanced diet for a dog is one in which all major food groups are present.

HOW MANY CALORIES?

The following serves as a guide when comparing calories in different food types:

Wet food contains 125 calories per 3.5 oz (100 g) = 600 calories in a typical 400g can.

Dry food contains 375 calories per 3.5 oz (100 g) = one average cup of food.

To help with calculating your own pet's needs, the following are basic calculations of energy output, ie. how many kilocalories are needed to sustain normal activity:

Typical energy requirements for 22 lb (small) dog:

Sedentary	610
Active dog	700
Working Dog	900
Older Dog (over 10 yrs)	500

Typical energy requirements for a 44 lb (large) dog:

Sedentary dog	1040
Active Dog	1180
Working Dog	1660
Older Dog (over 9 years)	850

Prepared Versus Home-Cooked Foods

This is a controversial area, with those favouring home-cooked foods emphasizing that they have much more control over the ingredients of their pet's food than those who choose commercially manufactured dog food. On the other hand, the massive worldwide pet food industry caters for the vast majority of dogs, which are now much healthier and have a longer life expectancy than at any stage in the past. Intensive research by and on behalf of these companies means that the nutritional requirements of domestic dogs are better understood than ever before, and so these manufacturers are ideally placed to use these findings to benefit the health of the dogs.

Conversely, there have been concerns about some of the ingredients that enter the pet food chain. However, if you stick with reputable brand names, you should not have any worries on this basis. Advocates of home-cooked foods point out that dogs generally prefer meals of this type when

SOME READY-MADE SPECIALIST DIETS

Lifestage
These cater for the changing nutritional needs of dogs from puppyhood to old age.

Breed-specific
An increasing number of diets aimed at specific breeds, such as German Shepherd Dogs and Bulldogs, are now available.

Vegetarian
Intended for all dogs, this is often a dry food and may cause increased flatulence at first.

Weight-loss
Sometimes called 'lite' food, this diet is more beneficial for obese rather than overweight dogs. It is available on prescription.

Working dog
These foods are intended for dogs that are highly active by nature, such as sled dogs.

Hypoallergenic
These diets are specially formulated for dogs that are known to be allergic to components of ordinary dog food.

Gluten-free
This is intended for dogs that are known to be allergic to gluten.

Pancreatic
This prescription diet is for dogs suffering from pancreatic insufficiency, which prevents them from digesting ordinary dog food.

offered a choice, but this does not necessarily mean that the food is better. A number of factors influence a dog's choice of food. For example, they are instinctively drawn to warm food, which is more reminiscent of freshly killed prey and has a similar texture (this also explains why it is possible to enhance the palatability of dry food by pouring a little hot water over it).

The biggest problem with using home-cooked food is that is can be difficult to calculate accurately how many calories you are providing in each meal. This assumes even greater significance when you are trying to reduce your dog's weight. There is also the drawback that you may not be able to source the specific ingredients added to commercial weight-reduction diets, such as insoluble fibre, making the task even harder.

Another vital area is meeting your dog's vitamin and mineral requirements. It is crucial that you feed your pet a balanced diet. Feeding prime steak, for example, will inevitably result in a deficiency of calcium in your pet's body, simply because that mineral is missing from this cut of beef. Using a ready-prepared food, formulated to exacting standards, takes away the guess-work of trying to work out which supplements are necessary to keep your dog in peak condition, while trying to reduce its weight.

It is often said that feeding a dog meat rather than proprietary dog food is healthier, but this is not necessarily true. Meat should be cooked and never fed raw, not because there is any truth in the story that dogs fed on raw meat are likely to be aggressive, but simply because the meat may be contaminated by a host of potentially harmful bacteria such as *Campylobacter*, *E. coli* and *Salmonella*, some of which could cause illness in your pet and possibly spread to you and other family members. This risk is not normally associated with canned or dry foods, unless they become contaminated from other sources.

CARBOHYDRATES AND WEIGHT-LOSS DIETS

The carbohydrate used in dog food is largely derived from cereal grains such as wheat and barley, which are cooked to improve their digestibility. Not all forms of carbohydrate can be digested by dogs, because unlike herbivores, they lack the ability to break down cellulose. However, indigestible carbohydrates are often incorporated into dog food as bulk, and can be of particular use when slimming down your dog.

Protein and Carbohydrate

In the wild, predators such as wolves feed mainly on meat, which consists of protein. However, commercial dry dog foods are comprised of 30–70 per cent carbohydrate. This is partly a reflection of manufacturing costs – carbohydrates are of vegetable origin and so are significantly cheaper ingredients than protein derived from meat. They can also add valuable structure to the food, particularly in the case of dry foods.

Using a significant amount of carbohydrate in a dog's diet is nothing new. In medieval times, stale bread rather than meat was the staple ingredient in the diets of packs of hounds. Wolves do in fact require carbohydrate as a source of energy, but the only natural elements of carbohydrate in their diet are likely to be derived from eating the intestinal contents of herbivores, which contain partially digested grass and herbage, or through fruits and berries. Unsurprisingly, therefore, wolves have the ability to convert protein in their diet into carbohydrate, to meet their energy needs and to utilize for growth and muscle repair. Dogs have inherited the ability to carry out this biochemical process. Prepared dog foods essentially circumvent the need for this process, by offering carbohydrate in a form that can be digested easily by the dog, in combination with a correspondingly lower level of protein.

COMPARING NUTRITIONAL VALUES

It is not easy to compare nutritional values between different types of dog food, such as dry and wet food. Wet food contains more water than dry food, so you need to work out the contents of the wet food without the moisture content, to compare the two.
- Subtract the moisture percentage from 100. If this is 78%, the dry matter would be 22%.
- If the food contains 10% protein according to the label, divide 10 by 22 = 45% protein on a dry matter basis.
- Repeat this for the fat content. If this is shown on the label as 8%, this translates to 36% of the dry matter.
- Finally, work out the carbohydrate content by adding the protein and fat figures together, then deducting them from 100, along with the ash percentage as shown on the can. If the ash content is 4%, for example, the calculation is 100 – 85. This means that the wet food contains 15% carbohydrate (notwithstanding moisture).

High-Fibre Diets

A diet that contains a relatively high level of dietary fibre will leave the dog feeling full after eating a meal, and can help to reduce the dog's appetite. In addition, a high proportion of fibre serves to lower the overall calorific value of food, so commercial weight-loss diets typically incorporate relatively high levels of fibre. Fibre included in pet foods is derived from a variety of plant sources. These typically include rice hulls, which are the external coating left after the grain itself has been removed, as well as soya bean hulls and bran; bran is sometimes added to home-cooked pet food for this reason.

A high-fibre diet is also beneficial for older dogs that may be prone to constipation because it helps to regularize the passage of food through the dog's digestive tract. It works by retaining water and increasing the bulk of the stool. In the colon, which is at the end of the digestive tract, some of this fibre may be broken down under bacterial influence to produce fatty acids. These can help to stabilize this part of the digestive system and prevent harmful bacteria from becoming established here.

Nevertheless, not all types of fibre are effective in terms of maintaining the overall health of the digestive tract. Effectiveness is linked to a characteristic that is often described as the rate of fermentation. Cellulose is one of the best sources of dietary fibre for treating obesity because it ferments slowly in the intestinal tract compared with soya bean fibre, for example, which ferments much more rapidly. Slow-fermenting fibres are less affected by the conditions in the intestinal tract and can hold more water, whereas those that ferment quickly cause increased gas production, leading to greater levels of flatulence and may have a laxative effect. In order to ensure a balance, dog foods therefore contain a mix of different types of fibre.

DIABETES AND HIGH-FIBRE DIETS

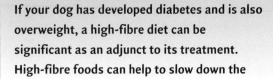

If your dog has developed diabetes and is also overweight, a high-fibre diet can be significant as an adjunct to its treatment. High-fibre foods can help to slow down the absorption of glucose after a meal, ensuring that there is not a sudden rush of glucose into the bloodstream which makes diabetes difficult to control.

Not All Fats are the Same

Although fat has a negative image these days, it is actually an important ingredient in a dog's diet and is beneficial to its well-being. The key is to ensure moderation. In cases of obesity, it is frequently not the fat component of the dog's diet that is the problem, but rather excess carbohydrate that is converted and stored in the body as fat. Dogs, like many other creatures, have developed the ability to lay down stores of fat in their bodies. This represents an efficient way of storing what is in effect surplus energy, being twice as concentrated in terms of calories as carbohydrate. Fat can have a protective function, too, protecting vital body organs such as the kidneys from trauma. It is also important

Dogs that live and work in cold climates, such as Arctic sled dogs, expend lots of energy, so they can cope with and actually benefit from a high-fat diet.

as a component of cell membranes, as well as for general health.

Fats are made up of a series of constituents known as fatty acids, some of which are essential because they cannot be manufactured in the body. There are a variety of sources of fat incorporated into commercial dog foods. These can include poultry fat and lard, which are of animal origin, as well as vegetable fats such as hydrogenated vegetable oils like corn oil. The essential fatty acid component of these different fats can vary widely. Corn oil, for example, contains more than double the level of linoleic acid found in poultry fat.

Essential fatty acids should constitute 1 per cent of a dog's daily diet, and commercial diets are made up so that there will not be a deficiency of this key dietary component, irrespective of the source of the fat. A shortfall can still arise, however, if you obtain a large bag of dog food that you fail to use up before the recommended use-by date on the pack – particularly if it is stored in direct sunlight, for example, where the heat is likely to turn the fat rancid. To safeguard your dog's health, store prepared food carefully, and always use it up before the expiry date.

As a concentrated source of energy, the fat level of the dog's diet should vary depending on its level of activity. A typical adult dog may require no more than 9 per cent fat in its diet, whereas, at the other extreme, a working sled dog in the Arctic may benefit from 50 per cent of its diet being fat, in order to meet its energy requirements and prevent loss of body condition.

To slim down an obese dog, a diet with a relatively low level of fat is needed. Weight-loss diets are formulated accordingly, but dogs on such foods can sometimes show signs of an essential fatty acid deficiency. If you are relying on a home-cooked weight-loss diet, it is recommended that you guard against this problem by supplementing the food with a little safflower oil, which is a very rich source of linoleic acid.

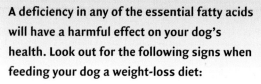

ESSENTIAL FATTY ACID DEFICIENCY

A deficiency in any of the essential fatty acids will have a harmful effect on your dog's health. Look out for the following signs when feeding your dog a weight-loss diet:
• Scurfy skin

• Dull-looking coat that has no lustre
• Increased incidence of skin infections
• Inability of a bitch to conceive if the dog's diet is low in essential fatty acids, such as linoleic acid.

The Effects of Fat on the Pancreas

Dogs that are fed an excessive amount of fat are at risk of developing pancreatitis, which results in inflammation of the pancreas. The pancreas is a gland that is located adjacent to the small intestine. Part of its function is to release enzymes that are vital for the digestive process through a duct into this part of the intestinal tract.

Pancreatitis can arise easily if you regularly feed your pet with the fatty off-cuts from meat. Middle-aged bitches are especially at risk, particularly if they are already overweight, and also suffering from diabetes mellitus (see page 82), which is a condition linked to both obesity and the pancreas.

As well as putting stress on the joints, obesity also affects a dog's internal organs. The longer obesity continues, the more damage is done.

Pancreatitis tends to be an illness more commonly found in smaller breeds, such as West Highland White Terriers, Miniature Poodles and Cocker Spaniels. It is a very painful condition, causing vomiting and diarrhoea. An affected dog will tend to lie down on its forelegs, while keeping its hindquarters raised, presumably as a way of trying to counter the pain. Blood tests are helpful in confirming the cause of this illness, with food then being withheld for about three days to allow the pancreas to recover without more challenges.

Subsequently, the fat content of your dog's diet will need to be significantly reduced. Table scraps, especially fatty trimmings off meat that might have triggered the illness in the first place, need to be cut out entirely. It may also help to prevent a recurrence if your dog's food is given in several small portions during the course of the day, rather than being offered in one or two large meals, thereby lessening the demands on the pancreas.

A possible long-term complication that can be associated with both pancreatitis and diabetes mellitus is exocrine pancreatic insufficiency (German Shepherd Dogs appear to have a genetic predisposition to this condition). Here, the pancreas loses its ability to produce the digestive enzymes necessary for the breakdown of dietary fat. In spite of having a large appetite, an affected dog will lose weight and suffer from a severe greyish diarrhoea, being unable to digest the fat present in its food. Treatment entails providing supplementary enzymes in the form of capsules to help the dog to digest its food more effectively. These will often control the deficiency successfully, but it is usually difficult to improve the dog's condition so that it regains weight.

Different Breed Requirements

When feeding a dog with commercially prepared food, it is important to bear in mind that the recommended amounts from the manufacturer are simply guidelines. A number of other factors are also significant in determining the correct quantity of food, the most important being your dog's level of activity.

In most cases the manufacturer's feeding instructions are likely to be on the generous side, to the extent that you may find that your dog puts on weight even if you stick strictly to the guidelines. This is because they are based on a dog's size, rather than taking any account of its age. Older dogs are likely to start putting on weight if fed at the recommended level, which may be more suited to younger dogs.

There may also be breed differences, which is an area of pet nutrition currently receiving increasing interest. At the very least, smooth, thin-coated breeds such as the Italian Greyhound are likely to require more energy simply to maintain their body temperature than breeds that have dense, weather-resistant coats like the Cairn Terrier, which were originally bred to work outdoors in a relatively harsh climate. Much of the work that dog food manufacturers originally

Cairn Terriers were originally bred for life outdoors, growing double-layer coats to help maintain their body temperature. As a result they need less food when kept in a warm home as a household pet.

carried out to determine the daily energy requirements of dogs was actually based on that of those housed in kennels, rather than dogs living a more sedentary lifestyle as pets within the home. Kennelled dogs tend to be more active throughout the day than pet dogs, which tend to be living in warmer conditions and so expend less energy maintaining their body temperature. As a result, the food requirements of kennelled dogs are greater than those of pet dogs, although this is not necessarily reflected in the manufacturer's feeding guidelines.

High Protein Levels and Older Dogs

Studies involving older dogs, which are the group at greatest risk of suffering from obesity, have shown that switching to a more natural diet can be particularly beneficial at this stage in a dog's life. Such a diet would contain a higher level of protein and less carbohydrate, similar to the diet of a wolf. As dogs grow older, their protein requirements increase, mirroring their requirements when younger. This helps to make up for wear and tear on the body, aiding recuperation from minor injuries. It has also been shown that using a food of this type can actually lead to improved weight loss, without having to reduce carbohydrate intake. This is the result of energy being derived from fat, without affecting muscle mass.

Remember that illness may impact on a dog's dietary requirements, especially towards the end of its life. Chronic renal failure, affecting the kidneys, means that elderly dogs often need special prescription diets as part of their treatment plan.

CELEBRATORY CEREAL CRUNCH

The fact that you are watching your pet's calorie intake does not mean that special events such as birthdays cannot be celebrated in style. Try this easy recipe:
• Crumble a wheat breakfast biscuit and two handfuls of bran flakes, then mix together.
• Stir 4 tablespoons of low-fat natural yoghurt into the crumble mixture.
• Spoon the mixture into your dog's bowl and decorate with slices of apple and carrot.

Exercising Your Dog

Wolf packs may roam across huge territories and often cover considerable distances in search of food. This does not require great speed – wolves tend to run only when pursuing their quarry, usually in packs – but it does demand great stamina, with the pack usually being constantly on the move.

As the domestication of the dog has progressed and their physique has changed from that of the wolf, so dogs' exercise needs have altered. Sighthounds, such as Greyhounds, with their athletic build, were bred for pace rather than the stamina of wolves, and breeds such as the Bulldog have now become increasingly less agile, when compared with their predecessors, so that they tend to amble along rather than actually run. The amount and type of exercise required by different breeds varies, depending on their anatomy.

Other factors, such as the age of the dog, are also significant. For example, it is important not to over-exercise giant breeds such as Great Danes or Irish Wolfhounds as puppies because this can lead to joint weaknesses later in life. Dogs tend to require less exercise as they age, although this depends to some extent on the individual and its state of health.

The problems of age are only compounded by obesity. Obese dogs are not able to tolerate as much exercise as slimmer dogs, particularly if also afflicted by medical problems such as chronic heart failure. Ideally, weight management should involve reducing calorie intake in combination with exercise, but if your dog is elderly and/or in poor health you will have to concentrate on diet as a way of controlling your pet's weight, rather than diet in conjunction with increased daily exercise.

Short-nosed breeds such as this Bulldog can get out of breath, particularly when exercising for long periods. Preventing obesity is key in these breeds.

How Much Exercise?

Regular exercise is much more significant in terms of keeping your pet fit and healthy than a marathon hike every weekend. Regular exercise tones the muscles and joints, helping to prevent strains and other injuries. In contrast, a dog that has not been out for several days and is then taken on a long walk is likely to run ahead at first, often proving to be less obedient while it uses up its surplus energy, and may finish up very tired at the end of the walk.

The length of walk depends partly on the breed. Some, such as Labrador Retrievers, benefit from longer walks; toy breeds such as Chihuahuas, can survive on less, though as a minimum they need to be taken out for at least half an hour each day.

If you want to know how far you have walked, a pedometer will give you some idea, but bear in mind that your dog will cover much more ground if it can run off the leash for at least part of the time. It will also help if you go out walking with a friend who has a dog, because your pets can then run together and take more exercise by chasing around with each other.

Giving your dog regular opportunities to run around is far healthier than only occasional exercise, when your pet is likely to run to exhaustion if unfit.

Taking a toy or ball out with you is another way to encourage your dog to exercise more actively. By engaging your dog's mind, you will find that your pet is more inclined to burn calories without it feeling like hard work.

WHY ARE BADLY TRAINED DOGS OFTEN OBESE?

A poorly trained dog is more likely to become obese than one that responds well to its handler when on a walk. Owners of such dogs worry that if they let their pets off the leash, their dog will run away and may be reluctant to come back when called. As a result, such dogs are not given as much exercise, and it can reach the point where they may not be taken out as frequently as they should be, even becoming obese.

As far as dogs are concerned, going out for a walk is not about keeping fit but about exploring the environment, in much the same way as a wolf wanders through its territory, investigating interesting scents and looking for food. It is important to vary your route if you can, to keep the dog's interest and prevent boredom, and it is important to keep your dog under control.

If you are worried about your dog's behaviour, you can seek the help of a professional dog trainer who can work with you on a one-to-one basis to deal with your pet's particular problems. Alternatively, sign up for a dog training course where other dogs will be present.

Time of Day

It is never a good idea to exercise dogs around midday in sunny weather when the temperature is at its hottest. This applies especially to obese dogs with thick coats because they can be especially vulnerable to the effects of hyperthermia. Dogs lack sweat glands to cool their bodies, relying instead on panting for this purpose. Many of the breeds that are most susceptible to becoming overweight, such as Boxers and Bulldogs, fall into the brachycephalic category, being characterized by their broad noses and short, compact faces. These dogs are far less able to regulate their body temperature by panting than breeds such as Greyhounds, simply because their nasal passages, from which water evaporates and takes heat from the body, are very short.

Develop a routine of exercising your dog in the morning and early evening when the temperature is cooler in order to reduce the likelihood of your pet collapsing from heat stroke. An obese dog is at increased risk of heat stroke because it is carrying more weight, which demands more energy and effort, so the dog is likely to be hotter as a consequence. This situation is even more dangerous in an elderly dog that is suffering from an underlying heart condition.

Weather

Dogs need exercise on a daily basis whatever the weather, not just to keep them fit, but also to prevent them from becoming bored and destructive around the home. Whatever the weather, make sure you keep up your dog's regular exercise pattern. However, when the weather is bad you may need to take some additional precautions before going out with your pet. Always try to take a mobile phone with you in case an accident happens and you need to summon assistance. This is important even if you walk in the same area on a regular basis, but especially if walking in unfamiliar areas.

In wet or cold weather, your dog may require a coat to keep warm, particularly if it is a short-coated breed such as a Whippet. There are various types of coat available, produced in different sizes. When deciding on the size most suitable for your pet, measure along your dog's back from the bottom of the neck to the base of the tail. If your pet is seriously overweight, consider the width of the strap that attaches around the body to hold the coat in place. It may be better in this case to choose a design that is attached by a sticky material fastener, as you will be able to adjust this

Basic obedience training is key to a solid owner/dog relationship. Your pet should come, sit and stay as instructed: crucial commands when out and about.

more easily than a button-up coat as your dog loses weight.

Depending on the prevailing weather conditions where you live, you may need two coats for your dog: a waterproof one for use on rainy days during the summer, and a thicker winter coat that offers greater protection against the cold.

The latter is particularly important for older dogs, because they can be reluctant to venture outside for any length of time if the weather is cold. The warm coat helps encourage them outside, where they will soon warm up on a walk.

Toys as Exercise Aids

If you exercise your dog on its own, take along a suitable toy that your pet can run after and retrieve in areas where it is safe to do so. It is obviously not a good idea to do this near roads, and also avoid throwing a toy for your pet in a park where other dogs are nearby. This could develop into a flash point, with another dog chasing after the toy and trying to steal it from your pet, leading to conflict.

Balls

Balls make excellent toys for dogs of all ages, and luckily, since dogs retain a playful side to their nature right through into old age, it should be possible to persuade your pet to exercise in this way through most of its life, albeit at a gradually slower pace as it ages. Running back and forth with the ball also means that a dog can cover twice as much ground during the course of a walk. This is a great way to give your pet more exercise even when time is short.

It is important to pick a ball that will be safe for your pet. Avoid using a hard ball because the dog may easily be injured if the ball hits your pet when

Taking a ball with you when you go out for a walk with your dog, particularly one that your dog plays with at home, will encourage your pet to get more exercise.

it is thrown or bounced. It is also important to choose a ball of suitable size so that it cannot be inadvertently swallowed; a dog can die if a ball becomes lodged in its throat. On the other hand, it helps to have a ball that is small enough so that your dog can pick it up and carry it easily.

Footballs are generally unsuitable for this reason, and once it has deflated slightly, the dog's sharp canines are likely to puncture the ball. Some dogs can become frustrated playing with a football if they cannot pick it up. This often causes them to run around pushing the ball along with their mouth open, barking loudly and repeatedly as they try to grab hold of it.

A brightly coloured ball is a good choice, simply because you may be able to spot it more easily in the undergrowth if your dog loses interest in the game. Although you can buy toy balls specifically intended for dogs, a tennis ball would do just as well. This is a suitable size for virtually all breeds and tends to stand out in grass because of its bright yellow in colour. Its slightly elastic nature means that even small dogs can pick up a tennis ball and carry it in their jaws without difficulty, and the ball will float if it rolls into water, making it easier to retrieve. Tennis balls are suitable on most surfaces, being easy to roll along a path. Bouncing dog toys are less satisfactory in areas where there is undergrowth nearby as they may fly off the track and can be hard to find.

Train your dog to drop the ball on command by simply walking away from it when he does not give it to you. He should not chase after other balls in the park, interfering in a children's game for example, which could give rise to complaints.

Throw a flying disc so that your dog has to run in order to catch it. Don't throw it directly at your dog, especially if it is the first time you've played with one.

Flying Discs

Flying discs are available in different diameters, making them suitable for dog breeds of all sizes to carry easily. These toys are ideal in areas of open country, with dogs such as Retrievers soon learning to chase after and even leap up and catch the disc in the air. Choose one of the designs sold specifically for dogs rather than the version that is a beach toy for humans. They tend to be made of softer material, which will not hurt the dog's mouth if your pet tries to catch the disc rather than picking it up from the ground.

Although they are most likely to appeal to younger dogs, older dogs will also chase after flying discs, particularly if a dog has been used to playing with a disc from an early age. In the case of less mobile dogs, always throw the disc so that it flies low to the ground, so your dog will not have to jump into the air to catch the disc, risking an awkward fall and injury, particularly if he is overweight.

HYDROTHERAPY SESSIONS

Hydrotherapy sessions for dogs are available in many areas. They are particularly good for older obese dogs. The water supports the dog so that it can swim easily, without its joints having to bear its full weight.

The warm water also helps prevent muscles seizing up. With regular sessions older obese dogs suffering from arthritis can build up fitness levels and lose weight despite not being able to walk long distances.

Swimming as Exercise

Walking and running are just two forms of exercise that benefit dogs, helping to prevent them from becoming overweight, or serving to curb their weight. Many dogs also enjoy swimming if given the opportunity. This applies particularly to breeds that were originally bred to work in water, such as the Labrador and other retrievers, as well as the Standard Poodle. Although its coat styling looks highly ornamental, the Poodle's distinctive trim was actually created for a functional purpose. The coat was left long over the body to provide insulation when the dog plunged into cold water to retrieve the hunter's quarry, while the area of fur around the joints was clipped to make it easier for the poodle to paddle and swim. A pompom of hair was left on the tail to make the dog easy to spot when swimming among reed beds, acting rather like a buoy.

Breeds of this type still retain a strong affiliation with water, jumping in readily when an opportunity presents itself, whereas thin-coated breeds such as the Whippet are often less inclined to take the plunge. However, swimming is a beneficial form of exercise for all dogs, particularly older dogs that have joint ailments that make running or even walking painful.

Potential Dangers of Water

If you are out walking with your dog, you will need to take care if it is a breed that is instinctively drawn to swimming in water. Not all localities are safe for this purpose. Avoid urban canals, for example, where the water may be polluted, or stagnant ponds, because the likelihood is that your dog may emerge covered in algae.

Choose river locations carefully, avoiding those where there is a strong current, or where the water is flowing over a nearby weir or waterfall downstream. It is also important to pick a stretch of riverbank where your dog can get in and out of the water easily. This ensures that if your pet becomes tired or cold, it can get back on to firm ground without difficulty. Dogs do not spend long in the water, usually preferring to splash around in the shallows, particularly when accompanied by another dog.

In some locations there can be hidden dangers lurking in the water. In most warmer parts of the world, such as the south-eastern region of the United States or northern Australia, crocodilians pose a threat to dogs. Dogs have no instinctive awareness of the danger posed by these hunters, and there is evidence that crocodilians target dogs in preference to other prey. Dogs can also be seized from the water's edge.

Take care not to let your dog splash about in water where there may be breeding birds present. Some of these, such as swans, can be fierce in defence of their nests and in a confrontation could easily injure a dog with their powerful wings.

Retrievers love the water and will readily fetch a toy if thrown in. Establish the safety of the area first.

VARY THE LOCATION OF EXERCISE

There are likely to be many locations where you can exercise your dog. If you do not have a car, it may be possible to take your pet farther afield on public transport, rather than just walking around the local park. New areas may have greater opportunities to run or swim, helping to increase your pet's fitness, and to lose weight.

Dangers on Land

Even on dry land, there are a number of potential dangers on land that you need to be aware of.

Farmstock

Train your dog not to disturb livestock when out. Otherwise, especially at lambing time, your dog could end up being shot for sheep-worrying by a farmer. It can also be dangerous for a dog to wander in a field of cattle that may become nervous. The problem is often greatest with dogs whose ancestors were bred to work with livestock, such as German Shepherd dogs, as the working instincts of such breeds remain strong. They are drawn to the sheep, but can be confused as to their role and may end up harrying them. Size is not always an indicator of a breed that may worry livestock. Corgis were once kept to herd cattle, nipping at their feet to move them along.

Snakes

Venomous snakes can be a hazard to dogs in many parts of the world, especially in the early part of the day when the temperature is cool and these reptiles are sluggish and less able to move. Rather than slip away undetected, they may strike with their fangs.

Prevent your dog from straying too far ahead in areas where venomous snakes may be present, so that you can intervene if necessary. If your dog is bitten, keep him as calm as possible to prevent the venom from spreading rapidly. If the bite is on a leg, tie a ligature across the top of the affected limb. This will need to be fairly tight, but not so firmly applied that it constricts the blood supply.

Where possible, photograph the snake if you do not recognize it. In a country such as Australia or North America, there may be a number of different venomous species present. In Europe it is the adder, with the highly distinctive zigzag patterning running down its back, that is the danger, being responsible for the deaths of a number of dogs each year. Take your dog to the nearest veterinary practice without delay for emergency treatment if it has been bitten by a snake, telephoning ahead if possible to warn them and tell them the type of snake if you can.

Ticks

Lyme disease occurs in many areas of the world, including the United States, much of Europe and northern parts of Australia. A bacterial infection, it is most frequently spread by ticks. Dogs and other animals, as well as people, are at risk of infection by walking through areas where ticks are, most commonly seen during the summer months, when they are active and looking for hosts. They will anchor on to the dog's body and inject the *Borrelia* bacteria with their mouthparts when they feed on their host's blood. Lyme disease affects the joints, although it can also cause signs of more generalized illness such as fever and weight loss. It can be treated with anti-biotics, which may be given as a precautionary measure when infection is suspected.

A number of similar illnesses can be transmitted by ticks living on wild animals such as deer. There are sprays that you can apply to your dog's coat to prevent ticks attaching themselves as your

WEIGHT-LOSS DIARY

The following is a programme that might help the average overweight medium sized dog meet a target weight that is 2% less than its current weight. Depending on whether it is the start of a weight-loss programme or nearer the end, the amount of actual weight loss per week will vary, with less being lost towards the end. Weight should be checked weekly:

Monday: Walked in the park for 20 minutes.

Tuesday: Good run on the heath, for an hour.

Wednesday: Just a walk down to the shops.

Thursday: Another walk in the park for 30 minutes. Did not run a great deal.

Friday: Back to the park. Walked for 30 minutes. Ran with Millie.

Saturday: Playing on the beach for 2 hours.

Sunday: Back to the heath for 2 hours.

Walked: (according to my pedometer reading) 15 miles (9.38 km)

EXERCISE PREFERENCES OF DIFFERENT BREEDS

- **Scenthounds (eg. Beagle):** A good run in the countryside.
- **Sighthounds (eg. Greyhound):** Often prefer running in short bursts in open countryside.
- **Sporting dogs (eg. Labrador Retriever):** Vigorous exercise, including swimming.
- **Utility dogs (eg. Rottweiler):** A good walk, but may not mix well with similar breeds.
- **Pastoral (eg. Old English Sheepdog):** Plenty of exercise, but take care to avoid contact with livestock.
- **Terriers (eg. West Highland White Terrier):** Happy walking and exploring in parks and the countryside, having good stamina.
- **Toys (eg. Pug):** Happy with a walk to the park and time off the leash there.

dog moves through grass or under-growth. If you have a small dog, you will need to treat more of its body than if it is a giant breed.

Check your dog's coat carefully for ticks at the end of each walk. They may not be conspicuous at this stage, because they do not swell until they have fed on your pet's body fluid, so you may only spot them later, such as when grooming your pet after a walk.

Ticks attach themselves firmly to your dog's skin with their powerful mouthparts, and cannot be removed easily. Sprays are available to persuade ticks to loosen their grip once they have attached to an animal, but the simplest method is to wipe the tick with a dab of petroleum jelly. This blocks off the breathing spiracle forcing the parasite to release its hold.

Fleas

Dogs are less likely to acquire fleas from being exercised in country areas than when walking in city parks, where they may come into close contact with other dogs, allowing fleas to jump from one dog to another. Once in the home, the adult fleas will lay their eggs in the dog's environment and those will hatch into minute larvae which pupate and new adult fleas emerge, the process often triggered by nearby movement. The flea then leaps up on to the dog, and thanks to their rapid reproductive rate, you can soon be facing an epidemic.

You should treat your dog routinely as a precautionary measure against fleas, particularly if he regularly comes into contact with other dogs. If there is also a cat in your home, the likelihood is that your cat will also need to be treated, as fleas may move across from pets. Bear in mind that flea treatments for dogs may not be suitable for cats.

Fleas tend to become more prevalent in the summer, although they can be a problem all year round in centrally heated homes. A neuro-transmitter inhibitor treatment is available as a preventative measure which interferes with the flea's nervous system and kills the parasites over a period of time. Some products of this type are also effective against ticks. Apply directly to the dog's skin as it drops; part the fur over the back of the neck to administer it.

If your dog has already acquired fleas, then an insect growth regulator (IGR) or an insect development inhibitor (IDI) is likely to be beneficial. Both of these treatments block the development of the eggs laid by female fleas, although they will not kill the adult parasites.

Chiggers

Repeated scratching is a common sign of fleas, but if your dog starts biting and chewing at its feet, this is may indicate another parasite, known as the harvest mite. This is so-called because it is only significant in late summer, when the parasitic larvae, known as chiggers, (rather than the free-living adult mites) cause a problem. These are likely to be picked up by a dog walking through a field or in long grass where the larvae are lurking.

Do not try to inspect your dog's feet too closely if it appears to be suffering from this condition, because the irritation is such that even a mild-mannered dog may snap. It is also hard to spot the tiny orange dots that are the larvae. Adult harvest mites resemble tiny bright red spiders. Seek veterinary advice for treatment.

Hookworm

In areas where dogs regularly exercise, such as public parks, there is the risk of a build-up of parasites in the soil. Regular preventative treatment is the best way of protecting your dog under these circumstances, with the prophylactic medication that is required varying from region to region. However, some parasites, such as hookworms, are more determined than others in gaining access to a host's body. They can be a particular problem for dogs in warmer climates, such as southern parts of the United States.

Exercising your dog in damp areas increases the risk of acquiring a hookworm infection, as this is where the larvae will survive, having hatched from their eggs. The immature hookworms then usually migrate into the intestinal tract, and can cause severe haemorrhaging. In areas where hookworm is present, the safest option is to give your dog a suitable deworming tablet regularly as a preventative measure, as advised by your vet.

Visiting a Beach

Offering the best of both worlds for running and swimming, many dogs enjoy exercising on a beach, particularly if it is sandy and they can run for long distances when the tide is out. There can be local restrictions on taking dogs onto beaches, however, and in fact it is better to take your pet to the beach for relatively short periods of time. There are a number of reasons for this. During

holiday periods when the weather is warm, there are likely to be many distractions that will require you to supervise your pet closely. On sunny days, there is also a risk that your dog could suffer from heat stroke. You must protect your pet by taking a suitable screen, such as a beach umbrella, and a towel for your dog to lie on. Always pack a bottle of drinking water and a bowl even if you are only planning a short visit, because your dog is likely to want a drink after a run but must not be allowed to drink seawater, which would be harmful.

Wide stretches of sand are great places to get fresh air and exercise in safety. First, make sure that dogs are allowed on to a particular beach at the time you wish to go, and always clean up after your dog.

Tide times are often published in local newspapers or can be found on the internet. These may show just high tide, with low tide occurring approximately six hours later. It is better to take your dog at low tide, when more of the

TAKE CARE IN WINTER

You may need to vary where you walk your dog in winter. Avoid any route near frozen water, particularly if your dog is a keen swimmer, because he might run off over the ice, which could then give way. This could be extremely dangerous, even causing drowning, as spending time in near-freezing water can result in hypothermia very quickly.

Similarly, do not be tempted to allow your dog to play on a beach in rough weather, because your pet could be carried off by a strong wave if it goes near the water's edge. Your dog could also be washed off a groyne or harbour wall into the sea.

Dogs do not understand the inherent dangers of such situations, particularly if they are not used to exercising in such locations, and should be carefully watched.

beach will be uncovered. Choose a sandy area if possible, and take a spare old towel so you can dry your dog after it has been playing in the sea, although many dogs will shake themselves vigorously after emerging from water and dry off quickly. When you get home, your dog will need a bath to wash out salt from its coat.

Take a ball for your pet to chase on the beach and never be tempted to throw pebbles instead. You might injure your pet, but your dog could also chip a tooth, particularly one of the long canines at the corners of the mouth, if he tries to crunch on a pebble. Worse still, he could swallow the pebble – many dogs do this each year and have to undergo surgery to remove such stones from their stomachs.

Dogs like to splash about in the surf rather than swim out any distance from the shore, but keep an eye on your pet when it is in the water. This is particularly important on a stretch of coast that you are not familiar with, as there may be strong currents or the sea bed may slope down sharply so that your dog suddenly finds itself out of its depth.

Another potential problem, particularly after stormy weather, may be tar on the beach, especially along the tideline, so keep your dog on a leash on this section of the beach. This will prevent your pet from scavenging on any unpleasant items that may have been washed up.

If your dog normally wears a leather collar and leash, it is a good idea to replace this with a nylon collar and leash for seaside trips as these will not be affected by the salt water. In contrast, leather will become stained with the salt and deteriorate as a result of exposure to seawater. Whatever collar you use, remember to attach an identity tag.

Lifestage Considerations

As with humans, dogs' bodies change as they pass through different stages of life, from puppyhood to old age. Each lifestage brings its own health issues, and obesity can both contribute to and be a result of these. You should monitor your dog's weight from the moment you get your pet, and be aware of the health issues your dog will face at different lifestages.

Starting out with a new puppy is an exciting time, and the likelihood is that you and other family members may spoil your new pet.

Remember that dogs are very much creatures of routine, and they can be as adept at training us as we think we are at training them. So, if you feed your puppy a piece of food from the table, you are likely to find that your new pet is there at every mealtime, looking soulfully at you for a tidbit. If ignored, the puppy may take more positive action to attract your attention, placing a paw on your leg or whining.

Similarly, if you start using treats as a training aid, you can soon find yourself being conditioned into having to take a packet of treats in your pocket each time you take your dog for a walk. It can then reach the stage where you are providing your pet with extra snacks throughout the day, on top of regular meals.

In the short term, as the puppy will burn off a lot of energy, the effects may therefore not be obvious. By adulthood, however, these feeding patterns will be firmly established and are likely to be difficult to break. If your pet is active and has plenty of opportunity to exercise, your dog may not initially become noticeably overweight. From middle age onwards, however, the legacy of a life of treats is likely to become apparent, and your dog's weight could start to increase rapidly.

Neutering

Physiological changes in the body following neutering can be a contributory factor to obesity in dogs, and this problem is becoming especially prevalent now that increasing numbers of owners are opting to have their pets neutered. The age at which dogs are neutered depends to some extent on the breed, because large breeds develop and mature more slowly than their smaller relatives. Irish Wolfhounds and other giant breeds are unlikely to be mature until they are two or even three years old, whereas small dogs may be sexually mature by a year old. There is an increasing tendency to neuter bitches early in life, before their first season, because this has been shown to make them less vulnerable to mammary tumours. There are, however, important implications in terms of weight gain.

The Beagle is a breed that is susceptible to both mammary tumours and obesity, so it needs plenty of exercise to prevent it becoming overweight.

The Benefits of Neutering

Although there is a slight risk attached to any surgery, neutering is generally a safe procedure. There is a low risk of complications, so that the advantages significantly outweigh the potential drawbacks. Neutering reduces a male dog's tendency to stray, and makes him less inclined to become involved in aggressive confrontations with other dogs. Known as castration, the surgery involves removing the dog's testicles, although cosmetic surgery is now available to avoid changing the appearance of the dog by replacing the testicles with implants.

Neutering of a bitch, known as spaying, is a more invasive operation because it involves opening the abdominal cavity to remove the ovaries and uterus. However, this surgery ensures that your pet will not have unwanted litters of puppies. In addition, her periods of heat, when she has an instinctive desire to mate, will cease and therefore she will not need to be carefully supervised at these times to ensure that she does not have a chance encounter with a male dog. In an unneutered bitch, periods of heat are likely to continue right through until the end of the dog's life, because there is no equivalent to the human menopause in dogs. Furthermore, there will be no risk of the potentially life-threatening condition of pyometra that results from an infection of the uterus (see page 88), and the risk of mammary tumours will be significantly reduced.

Neutering and Weight Gain

Neutering has a significant impact on the body's hormonal balance and in turn on a dog's behaviour. Male dogs lose their interest in wandering off after bitches, or mounting their owner's leg, because the levels of the hormone testosterone in their bodies declines after neutering. Bitches no longer try to escape when in heat because their ovaries, which helped to produce the oestrogen hormone to stimulate sexual desire, have been removed.

Both testosterone and oestrogen serve to increase the dog's level of activity, so it is not surprising that a dog needs fewer calories to maintain its weight after being neutered. You therefore need to reduce your pet's food intake, possibly by up to a third, in order to prevent any significant increase in weight. Always monitor your dog's weight very closely after such surgery to detect early signs of unwanted weight gain, taking steps to remedy this before it develops into a major problem.

If you allow your dog to pile on extra pounds after being neutered, it will be much harder to get your pet back into shape when it approaches middle age. This is the stage at which a dog's level of activity starts to decline naturally, so feeding your pet the same amount of calories as when younger will inevitably lead to weight gain, and this will obviously be worse if your pet is already overweight after neutering.

Joint Problems

The extra weight that an obese dog carries, particularly when old, will put its joints under greater pressure when supporting and moving its body. The joints are likely to develop signs of wear, which makes moving painful, to the extent that your dog may be reluctant to exercise for any length of time, making it significantly harder to get your pet back into shape. If you can manage to reduce your dog's weight, however, the strain on the joints will be eased and the dog's physical condition will improve. Unfortunately, some breeds are susceptible to joint weaknesses such as hip dysplasia, which will be worsened if the dog is overweight.

Hip Dysplasia

This is an inherited condition, the incidence of which has been reduced by screening breeding stock, although it has not been eliminated.

Larger breeds, especially German Shepherd dogs, are especially at risk. The problem relates to the structure of the hip joint itself, which is often described as a ball and socket joint. Signs can emerge at quite a young age, and will be evident from x-ray images of the hip joints.

The ball-like head of the femur bone, at the top of each hind leg, should fit snugly into the cup formed by the hip, called the acetabulum. This helps to provide support for these limbs, which are well muscled and so provide the dog with power when it runs. In cases of hip dysplasia, the joint is significantly weakened, often because the cup is too shallow to provide adequate support for the head of the femur.

If the dog is overweight it becomes even more painful, because the hips are major weight-bearing joints, and so the stress on them will be markedly increased.

Torn Ligaments

It is not only the joints that will be creaking in an obese dog, but also the supporting ligaments. Although fibrous by nature and therefore relatively tough, ligaments can be sprained or even torn, especially if a dog is unfit. This can occur almost spontaneously – your dog does not need to be running at the time. Worse still, it may not just be the ligament itself that is damaged, but also the capsule of the joint itself.

The ligament that supports the dog's stifle joint – equivalent to our knee joint – is particularly at risk of being injured when a dog is obese. Certain breeds, notably Boxers but also Golden Retrievers, are especially prone to this problem. This may be linked with the angle created by the tibia, on the lower aspect of the joint, with studies suggesting that if this exceeds 28 degrees, an injury of this type will be more likely.

If the ligament snaps, rather like a rubber band, your dog will suddenly become lame and will be reluctant to put any weight on to the affected leg, because the support provided by the ligament is no longer present. The dog is therefore likely to start hobbling, although it will not be in a great deal of pain.

What to Do

Once a torn ligament injury has occurred, it is critical that the dog is placed on a diet if it is overweight. The injury itself can be confirmed by an x-ray image, and the dog is likely to need an operation to repair the ruptured ligament. If left, the dog's condition may improve gradually, but it will never regain the same range of movement in the joint as before the injury.

Surgery can lead to a much better recovery, but this is a slow process and is likely to take months. Physiotherapy can be beneficial during this phase, helping the dog to regain full use of the joint. There can be lasting complications, however, especially if the joint capsule itself was damaged.

Osteoarthritis, sometimes called degenerative joint disease (see page 78), is commonly linked with torn ligament injuries. In some cases, osteoarthritis may be evident on the x-ray pictures taken immediately after the ligament ruptured. This tends to suggest that the ligament had already been damaged previously, although it did not actually tear at this earlier stage. Unfortunately, signs of osteoarthritis will complicate the healing process.

Slipped Discs

Back problems are another area in which obesity can have severe consequences on your dog's skeletal structure. Some breeds, such as Dachshunds, already have a propensity to back problems because of an underlying weakness. These dogs have short legs and correspondingly elongated backs. Adding extra weight to the body can increase the flexion in the spinal column, placing greater pressure on the intervertebral discs that separate and cushion the vertebrae.

If the hard fibrous coating around the soft jelly-like core of the disc ruptures, this puts direct pressure on the spinal cord and the associated nerves that branch off and pass out from the vertebral column. The symptoms associated with a slipped disc depend on which part of the spinal cord is affected. More than one disc is often affected at the same time.

What to Do

Slipped discs are more likely to arise in dogs from middle age onwards because the discs themselves start to harden with age, making them more likely to rupture. Rapid veterinary treatment, usually involving the administration of corticosteroids that act as anti-inflammatory agents, can help to decrease the swelling and therefore aid healing.

If your dog slips a disc, it is vital to keep him as calm, still and quiet as possible, to allow healing to take place. Running around, which will inevitably entail sudden movements, will severely hamper the healing process. This imposed lack of activity creates the potential problem of your dog putting on additional weight during this crucial recovery period. It is therefore a good idea to switch your dog to a weight-reducing food with a high fibre content and rest. If rest does not prove satisfactory, the only other option for repairing slipped discs is surgery.

Preventing a Recurrence

Once a dog has suffered from a slipped disc, there is a likelihood that it will be affected again at some point in the future. It is therefore important that you take steps to minimize the risk. In addition to slimming your pet down to its target weight, you can reduce the risk of recurrences by preventing your dog from jumping up, whether on to a chair or into a car. You should also aim to stop your pet from climbing steps or stairs, because both these activities will put increased stress on the spinal column.

Dogs' joints come under a significant amount of wear-and-tear during their daily activities and their diet must be regulated to support this.

Osteoarthritis

The joints of all dogs are subject to wear, and because dogs are now living longer than at any stage in the past, chronic signs of inflamed joints are increasingly common. There is a clear link between osteoarthritis and obesity, and it is the major weight-bearing joints, particularly the hips, that are at risk. The signs vary, although often the earliest indication will be that your dog appears stiff on waking in the morning. You may also notice that your pet becomes less enthusiastic about jumping up, because of the strain and resulting pain that this imposes on the hip joints.

There is no treatment for osteoarthritis, but it can make a big difference to your dog's quality of life if you help your pet to slim down. This should hopefully serve to reduce your pet's dependence on painkillers as well, which can have harmful side effects. There is also the risk that painkillers could lead your dog to overexert itself when the pain has been temporarily numbed. This is then likely to worsen the situation in the longer term.

Cause of the Problem

At the surface of a joint, each bone is protected by a substance called cartilage which protects the ends of the bones from rubbing against each other. The joint is also encased with a synovial

Dachshunds are prone to slipped discs, due to their long bodies and short legs. Such problems can be severely worsened by osteoarthritis and obesity.

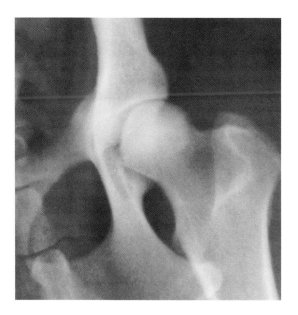
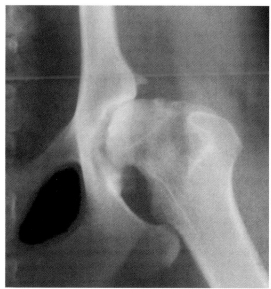

The image on the left shows a normal ball-and-socket hip joint; the image on the right shows pitting on the head of a femur suffering from osteoarthritis.

membrane that produces a fluid to lubricate the cartilage and protect it from damage, forming the inner part of the joint capsule. Where there is a problem with the structure of the joint, which may be linked to the dog's weight, the bones may no longer align properly. As a result, the surfaces may come into direct contact and rub against each other, eroding the protective spongy cartilage as a consequence.

Worse still, injured cartilage produces enzymes that will damage it further, rather than allowing the tissue to heal. The synovial membrane can also be damaged by the enzymes, as waste matter cannot be neutralized by the cartilage and builds up here. As the pain increases, your dog will become less enthusiastic about moving. This will further worsen the situation, because if the joint is largely immobile, the lubricating fluid is not being spread over its surface, causing greater damage and pain.

What to Do

It is important that you do not stop exercising your dog if it is suffering from osteoarthritis. Aside from aiding weight loss, exercise will stop your pet from suffering loss of muscle tone and overall fitness. Do not encourage your dog to undertake exercise such as chasing after a ball or jumping, however, because this places unnecessary strain on the joints.

The best solution is to take your pet out for short walks several times each day. If the weather is cold or wet, it is also a good idea to give your dog a coat to help keep its body warm, keeping the muscles toned more effectively as a consequence. Another option to consider is hydrotherapy (see page 64), which will allow your pet to exercise without causing pain to the joints.

You will also need to make some lifestyle changes so that your dog is more comfortable and less likely to overexert itself. Do not encourage your pet to jump up in your vehicle when you are going out for a walk. There are now special ramps available to allow your dog to get into vehicles, even high SUVs, without difficulty.

In the home, you may need to fit a child gate at the bottom of the stairs to deter your dog from trying to clamber up. Remember that the hip joints can be painful if the dog is suffering from osteoarthritis, so take great care when lifting and handling your pet. Otherwise, you could find that your dog snaps at you unexpectedly, and aside from the risk of being bitten yourself, you may drop your dog and cause further injury.

Dietary Help

As far as your pet's diet is concerned, it is not just losing weight that will counter the effects of osteoarthritis, but also the addition of joint-protecting substances in its food. Substances called chrondroprotectants have been identified, with initial research having focused on a compound present in New Zealand green-lipped mussels (*Perna canaliculus*), called glycosaminoglycan. Synthetic variants of this chemical have been manufactured and given by injection to help stimulate the regeneration of damaged cartilage. They may also have anti-inflammatory properties, lessening the pain linked with the condition, and have been shown to curb the release of enzymes by the body when cartilage is damaged.

This type of treatment can lead to a distinct improvement in your dog's condition, whereas pain relief by drugs simply relieves the symptoms by decreasing the inflammation. There are also a number of side effects linked with the use of non-steroidal anti-inflammatory drugs, ranging from stomach irritation to liver damage. However, by helping the joint to regenerate, even if this is only to a limited extent, you will be able to exercise your dog more, within limits, helping it to slim down as necessary and improve its condition accordingly.

Looking after a young dog's health is paramount in preventing a life-long tendency to obesity – which can occur as a result of too many fat cells in the body, as occurs in overweight puppies.

Pet food manufacturers have now introduced joint-protector substances to their foods. It is thought that maximum benefit may be gained from using these supplemented diets throughout the dog's life, particularly in the case of larger breeds that may be more prone to joint damage than their smaller counterparts. Supplements of this type are also included in senior rations, however, so it is never too late to take advantage of this type of food. Supplements are available in tablet form, based on glucosamine hydrochloride and chondrotin sulphate.

Another type of chrondroprotector has also been isolated from green-lipped mussel tissue. This is known as eicosatetranoic acid (ETA), and is an omega-3 fatty acid that has yet to be identified in any other species. It is thought to be very effective at reducing joint inflammation.

RELATIVE AGES IN DOGS

	Middle age	Elderly	Geriatric
Small (under 20 lb)	ca. 7 yrs	ca. 11 yrs	ca. 15 yrs
Medium (20–50 lb)	ca. 7 yrs	ca. 10 yrs	ca. 14 yrs
Large (over 50 lb)	ca. 5 yrs	ca. 9 yrs	ca. 12 yrs

COMPLEMENTARY REMEDIES

Some complementary treatments, notably acupuncture, practised for thousands of years in China, appear to help some cases of osteoarthritis (see page 78). Although the mechanism as to how it works is unclear, it seems that it may act as a stimulant, triggering the release of the body's natural painkillers, called endorphins, into the central nervous system. By relieving the pain in this way, there is a greater opportunity for healing to occur, resulting in a permanent improvement in the dog's condition. If you have a pet insurance policy, check to see if it includes cover for this type of treatment.

Diabetes

Another illness that has become much more prevalent in dogs over recent years, (as it has in people), is diabetes mellitus, also known as sugar diabetes. About 1 in every 200 dogs now suffers from diabetes, with bitches being at significantly greater risk of developing this illness than male dogs. Once again, obesity appears to be a predisposing factor, although some breeds such as Golden Retrievers and Dobermanns also seem naturally more vulnerable to diabetes than others.

The cause of the problem lies in a gland called the pancreas, which is located close to the small intestine. The pancreas releases the hormone insulin into the blood stream, which triggers cells to take up glucose. If there is a shortage of insulin, however, the cells are deprived of their source of energy, which then accumulates in the blood stream and gives rise to a high blood sugar level. This is known as Type 1 diabetes. If there is a plentiful supply of insulin but the cells simply do not respond to it, this is referred to as Type 2 diabetes.

Fat dogs are considered at a greater risk of developing diabetes because of the way in which the fat cells in their body expand in size. The resulting stress then causes increased output of a substance called cortisol from the adrenal glands located near the kidneys, which has the effect of preventing the fat cells from responding to insulin. As a result, obese dogs are most vulnerable to Type 2 diabetes. If your dog has become overweight, slimming may help to control the situation.

A simple urinary test can give an indication of whether your dog has diabetes, because some of the high level of glucose circulating in the blood, will be lost in the urine. Increased thirst and a correspondingly high urinary output is another clear symptom of this condition.

Obese dogs, such as these two Bull Mastiffs, are most vulnerable to diabetes.

FEMALE DOGS AND DIABETES

Bitches are more susceptible to diabetes than male dogs. This may be linked to a quirk sometimes seen in their metabolism when they are coming into heat.

You may notice that your pet starts to drink much more at this stage, and a blood test taken now would be likely to reveal increased blood sugar levels because the cells become temporarily unresponsive to insulin – just as occurs during Type 2 diabetes. This is probably the result of stress, causing an

output of cortisol from the adrenal glands. Once this transient phase has passed, these signs should disappear, but they do indicate that your pet could be more susceptible to diabetes. You should watch her weight closely and slim her down before the next period of heat – normally about six months later.

Assuming she is otherwise healthy, it may be better to have her neutered beforehand to avoid this situation arising.

What to Do

In the case of Type 2 diabetes, it may be possible to manage the condition primarily by controlling your pet's weight and feeding a suitable diet. Considerable research has been carried out over recent years to discover how dietary modifications can help to even out the absorption of sugars from the digestive tract. This avoids the sudden peak in glucose that may otherwise occur after a dog has eaten a meal, triggering a correspondingly high insulin rise before both fall back in sequence again.

Different carbohydrates are broken down into glucose at different rates, so this affects their rate of absorption into the blood stream. Rice is broken down very quickly into glucose, while at the other extreme barley is digested at a much slower rate. This means that by adjusting the different sources of carbohydrate in a dog's food, it is possible to ensure a more even demand for insulin.

The fibre content of the diet is also important, partly because this can decrease the dog's hunger pangs. As fibre swells up in the digestive tract, it draws in water, creating a sensation of fullness. Fibre can trap sugars, slowing the rate of absorption of glucose across the intestinal wall into the blood stream and helping to prevent a sudden rapid peak in demand for insulin after a meal. The use of high-fibre diets can also aid weight loss (see page 50), which is important in controlling diabetes. If you have been feeding your dog on semi-moist food, switch to another diet if diabetes is suspected because such foods

On-going veterinary check-ups are necessary for a dog which suffers from diabetes, although slimming him down can help to minimise the effects of this illness once it has been diagnosed.

use relatively high levels of sugar as a preservative. Although a dog will lose weight rapidly if it has diabetes, do not delay taking your dog to the vet because the side effects of waiting to obtain treatment are likely to be very serious. Cataracts are a particular problem, causing blindness that can only be relieved by surgery, although dogs do adapt to loss of vision better than humans as they are less reliant on this sense. In some cases, you may need to be prepared to give your dog regular insulin injections twice a day for the rest of its life to stabilize the condition. This is not as daunting as it sounds. The injections are given using a very fine needle in the scruff of the neck, so most dogs are unaware of them. It is important to stick to a stable feeding regime once the condition has been stabilized to minimize the risk of any complications. Specially formulated diets for diabetic dogs are available on veterinary prescription and these can provide the best feeding option under such circumstances. You must persuade young members of the family not to offer tidbits, or leave items such as sweets lying around in the home where your dog could steal them, because these could have serious effects on your pet's blood sugar levels.

Medical Causes of Increased Weight

Not all cases of weight gain in dogs are necessarily due to overfeeding combined with lack of exercise. If you find that your dog is gaining weight unexpectedly, especially from middle age onwards, arrange a veterinary check-up just in case your dog is ill.

There have been recent suggestions that viral infections by certain members of a group known as adenoviruses may be linked with cases of obesity, both in people and animals. This research is only just beginning, so any link between viral infections and well-defined causes of obesity, such as overfeeding and lack of exercise, have yet to be clearly worked out. It may turn out that a virus could trigger obesity by affecting the functioning of the body in some way, possibly by altering its metabolism and so causing a dog to gain weight.

Hypothyroidism

The most common medical cause of weight gain in dogs is the illness known as hypothyroidism, which affects the thyroid glands. These are found in the neck, lying very close to the windpipe. They produce thyroid hormones, which are chemical messengers carried around the body in the bloodstream, affecting the body's metabolic rate.

In cases of hypothyroidism, the thyroid glands are progressively destroyed by the dog's own immune system. The underlying cause of this reaction is unclear at present, and it is in this context that a virus might be implicated. As a direct result of damage to the thyroid glands, the output of thyroid hormones falls, giving rise to a wide range of clinical symptoms, including weight gain. Hypothyroidism tends to become most evident in dogs from middle age onwards, and the

signs may initially be confused with signs of aging itself.

You will notice that your dog starts to gain weight in spite of the fact that you are not giving it more food than usual. The dog also becomes less active, and is no longer as enthusiastic about going out for walks as before. There can also be a range of other signs, with affected individuals often feeling the cold more than normal, to the extent that they may shiver. Changes to the skin are most likely to suggest that something is wrong. The hair often becomes thinner than in the past, while the skin itself becomes thicker and minor skin infections may develop.

A blood test can easily diagnose this illness, with a raised cholesterol level and a fall in the numbers of red blood cells being present in the majority of cases, causing anaemia and helping to explain your pet's lethargy. The blood picture is also likely to show a raised level of thyroid-stimulating hormone, which reveals that the body is attempting to boost the hormonal output from these glands, while the level of the hormones themselves in the blood will be lower than normal.

In spite of the wide range of symptoms, treatment of hypothyroidism is straightforward. You will simply need to give your dog a synthetic form of the hormone known as L-thyroxine on a daily basis. Within a month, you should notice

Unexplained lack of energy, weight gain or weight loss may all indicate your pet has an illness and should be taken to a vet for diagnosis.

that your dog is returning to its old self, becoming more active and lively, and starting to lose weight. Even the changes in the coat and skin will be reversible, although this tends to take slightly longer to become noticeable.

Cushing's Disease

Hormonal problems can result in behavioural changes, such as a change in your dog's appetite. In the case of Cushing's disease, which affects the adrenal glands located near the kidneys, one of the most obvious signs is that your dog appears constantly hungry, gulping down its own food and stealing more whenever possible. The dog also develops a swollen belly. This is not a reflection of weight gain but rather the result of muscular weakness. The most evident sign of the condition is hair loss, which is even distributed on both sides of the body. The cause in this case can be a tumour, or is sometimes linked with the use of corticosteroids to treat other ailments.

Fluid Build-up

Sometimes a dog's abdomen may start to swell up and your pet appears to put on weight, although the cause is again not down to diet. Instead, it is caused by ascites, which in essence is a build-up of fluid in the abdomen. It is usually possible to determine this by tapping this part of your dog's body gently. This results in a dull noise, and you may feel a pressure wave reverberate across to the other side of the abdomen as the fluid moves. There are a number of potential causes of ascites, so you will need to consult your vet for advice and treatment.

False Pregnancy

You may also notice that a female dog starts to put on weight unexpectedly after her season. Assuming that she did not mate during this period, this is likely to indicate a false pregnancy, with hormones in her body suggesting that she is pregnant and even creating the signs of pregnancy, including the production of milk, with her nipples becoming swollen. You may also notice that she becomes very protective towards her toys, with her maternal instincts convincing her that they are her puppies. This phase should soon pass, but it is sensible to have her neutered afterwards, because false pregnancies frequently recur at subsequent heats.

Pyometra

A more sinister cause of weight gain linked with the female's reproductive cycle is pyometra. This is the result of an infection in the uterus. In some cases, there may be an unpleasant discharge from the dog's vulva, but in the case of what is described as closed pyometra, her abdomen can become swollen because the infective material remains trapped. Another early sign of this problem is that she will be excessively thirsty, and before long will have lost her appetite. This is an emergency situation, with pyometra itself being a potentially fatal condition, so you will need to seek veterinary advice without delay if you suspect that your dog could be suffering from this illness.

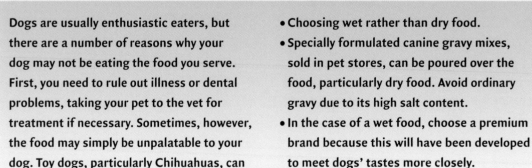

IMPROVING THE PALATABILITY OF FOOD

Dogs are usually enthusiastic eaters, but there are a number of reasons why your dog may not be eating the food you serve. First, you need to rule out illness or dental problems, taking your pet to the vet for treatment if necessary. Sometimes, however, the food may simply be unpalatable to your dog. Toy dogs, particularly Chihuahuas, can be fussy eaters. There are a number of things you can do to encourage your dog to eat. These include the following:

- Choosing wet rather than dry food.
- Specially formulated canine gravy mixes, sold in pet stores, can be poured over the food, particularly dry food. Avoid ordinary gravy due to its high salt content.
- In the case of a wet food, choose a premium brand because this will have been developed to meet dogs' tastes more closely.
- Do not feed food straight from the fridge; dogs prefer warm food.

Planning for Fitness

When dealing with the issue of canine obesity, one of the hardest things to do is to face up to the fact that your dog is overweight. If you are wavering about taking action, reflect on the fact that your dog is dependent on you to do so and is helpless to do anything itself. You must take positive action to see an improvement in your dog's condition – your pet will not lose weight without your help.

Do not confuse indulging your pet with treats with showing it affection, and do not worry that stopping giving your pet treats will cause the dog to withdraw from you altogether. This will simply not happen. Dogs may be easily bribed with treats, but your pet will not be any less pleased to see you when you come home at the end of the day if you abandon your practice of sharing a biscuit. Dogs are incapable of bearing grudges. The dog may show some signs of missing the treat at first, whining perhaps, but this phase will pass within a few days, particularly if you do not have a biscuit yourself.

Rest assured that your relationship with your pet will not suffer as a result of cutting back on treats or on the quantity of food that you offer at meal times. Indeed, once your dog starts to benefit from losing weight, you are likely to be rewarded with a more lively, energetic and enthusiastic companion who can share your life more fully, so helping your pet lose weight will benefit you both.

Life-Changing Situations

For some pet owners, it takes a life-changing moment to force them into confronting their pet's condition. There is the issue of pregnancy, for example. Obese bitches are more likely to encounter difficulties giving birth than those that are fit and healthy, but by this stage it will be too late to slim her down without the risk of harming the developing puppies.

Unless everything proceeds entirely smoothly during the birth, your dog may be at real risk,

because if labour proves to be problematic and medical treatments fail to work, a Caesarean section may be necessary, both to safeguard the bitch's health and that of her puppies. This can create on-going difficulties in terms of rearing the puppies, with further complications likely if she becomes pregnant in the future. In the worst-case scenario, you may have to hand-rear the puppies for a time, until the mother has recovered sufficiently to take over their care.

Heart Failure and Weight

Another common situation that will make it impossible to ignore the piled-on pounds is if your dog develops signs of heart failure. In contrast to humans, dogs rarely suffer a serious heart attack resulting from a blockage of the coronary arteries that supply the heart muscle with blood. Instead, dogs are more likely to develop congestive heart failure as they grow older, because of problems with the pair of valves that connect the four chambers in the heart.

This weakness means that some blood seeps backwards through the left ventricle, into the atrium for example, rather than being forced into the aorta and then around the body under pressure. A leaky valve means that the heart pumps less efficiently, having to do more work to expel the blood. Obesity can be a significant predisposing factor, forcing the heart to undertake more work pumping blood around

Helping an obese dog lose weight will put it in a better position to recover from illness, if medical problems put constraints on exercise later in life.

the body. This is particularly serious in breeds such as the Cavalier King Charles Spaniel that are prone to congenital heart weaknesses because of valvular defects, as well as obesity.

If your dog has damaged heart valves, which your vet is likely to be able to pick up simply by listening to the heart with a stethoscope, this should serve as a warning in regard to the dog's weight. Provided that the dog is not showing any signs of heart failure, it can live a normal life, being taken out for walks and encouraged to run as usual. If signs of clinical obesity follow, however, this may tilt the balance, causing your dog to suffer signs of heart failure, such as becoming tired very quickly as the result of exercise. Before long, your dog is likely to develop a dry cough that will often be heard after it has been out for a walk, or especially at night.

This is the stage at which medical treatment is required, and although it can be successful in terms of improving the ability of the heart to pump blood, you will need to change your dog's lifestyle as well, cutting back on walks. This presents a real difficulty if your dog is also overweight. The likelihood of being able to reduce your pet's weight by increasing its level of exercise will simply not be feasible.

You will need to rely more heavily on strict dietary control, although you can still take your dog out for walks. Instead of one long walk though, it may be better to split the exercise into several shorter walks, while taking care not to overtire your pet. It is important to come up with an action plan with realistic weight-loss targets because helping your pet to lose weight will assist your dog's overall state of health.

Accidental Weight Gain

Sometimes a dog becomes handicapped as the result of an accident, either with a short-term injury such as a broken leg, or a long-term problem such as losing a limb. Clearly, being confined while the injury is healing means that your dog's energy needs will be reduced, so a change in diet is advisable in order to reduce the number of calories your pet is getting. Otherwise, your dog may start to put on weight while immobilized, which could slow the rehabilitation process. Often in the trauma of the moment, it is easy to overlook the dietary changes that are needed, but discuss this with your veterinarian at an early stage. Even a fit dog is likely to gain weight under these circumstances, and this needs to be prevented as far as possible.

Getting Help

In situations where an overweight dog has an underlying health problem, it can be especially valuable to work with a veterinary practice that runs a weight-loss clinic. These types of clinic are growing in number due to the increased incidences of obesity. Rather than just improving your pet's weight through dieting and exercise, the clinic can devise an individual programme that takes account of your pet's pre-existing medical condition, ensuring that there are no adverse consequences from the weight-reduction plan.

Veterinary clinics of this type are held on a regular basis, giving the opportunity for medical check-ups and further investigations if there are any signs of concern. Just as importantly, you will be comforted in the knowledge that you are doing the best for your pet, whereas without this advice you may be reluctant to make the necessary lifestyle changes to your dog's routine, such as taking your pet for longer walks, in case something happens to cause the medical condition to worsen.

A dog can easily put on weight when confined due to injury unless you modify your pet's diet to reflect the reduced amount of exercise being taken.

Addressing Bad Habits

While an adult dog will never be as sprightly as when it was a puppy, once your pet is close to its target weight, you will be able to enjoy playing games and going for longer walks again. It really is possible to give a middle-aged dog a new lease of life if you can get it to shed those unwanted pounds. Ultimately, you have to engineer this yourself, and break some of the bad habits that your dog has acquired from you down the years.

Think carefully about how you reward your pet and its relationship with food. Some people worry that depriving their dog of treats or tidbits will

Hard as it may be not to give in to your pet's imploring eyes, you must resist overindulging him.

BE STRONG

It is perhaps easy to forget that you, the owner, must take ultimate responsibility for your dog's condition. Regular attendance at veterinary weight-loss clinics can help, by providing a real incentive to stick to the diet plan. Without this support, it is easy to succumb to those woeful eyes looking at you for a regular tidbit or leftovers at meal times, which will have contributed to the problem in the first place. If you want to improve your dog's condition, you will need to be firm with yourself as well your pet.

Whenever it becomes difficult, reflect back to when your dog was a puppy; jog your memory if necessary by looking at some old photographs of your dog at this early stage in its life. Weight gain is insidious and, until you see this with your own eyes, you probably will not realize just how much your pet's condition has deteriorated over the years. Obviously, you see that your dog has gained weight, but you may not be aware of just how its physique and level of activity has changed as a result.

weaken their relationship with their pet. Dogs do not judge their relationship with us in such terms. While it may be difficult to break a particular habit, this will not have a significant impact on your dog's relationship with you.

Supplementary feeding in the form of treats or tidbits, and/or the provision of too much food at meal times are both prime causes of obesity. Cutting out the unnecessary feeding between meals will help to address the weight problem and will not affect your dog's behaviour in the long run. Your pet may whine and follow you for a few

Most dogs love company and develop a close relationship with their pack members. Overfeeding is no substitute for spending time with your pet.

moments as a way of trying to remind you, thinking that you may have forgotten, but this phase will soon pass.

It is actually quite easy to break bad habits by varying your routine when you cut out the treats. If you always gave your dog a treat when you cleared the plates at the end of a meal, for example, change your routine by simply piling the plates up on the table and doing something elsewhere in the home for a period of time. Better still, take your dog out into the garden and play a game there, or go for a short stroll with your pet around the block. This will take the dog's mind off the situation by providing something else that is appealing. Dogs adapt very well to changes in routine. Just consider how a new dog settles into the home within a few days, often having just been separated from its mother. Simply not offering treats and tidbits is nothing like a change of this magnitude.

Adjusting Your Relationship

Time is precious nowadays, so if your dog is overweight, consider that you may be overcompensating for not spending enough time with it by offering treats instead, and overfeeding on demand. Try to judge this honestly. For example, when you take your dog out for a walk, do you follow the same route every day, often rushing to get back because you have things to do? It may well be that the initial excitement of having a dog has dissipated, not because you do not care for your pet, but simply because it has become a routine, perhaps even a rather dull part of your life.

This is where the other side of the obesity equation is relevant. Weight loss is achieved most effectively through a combination of a reduction in food intake and increased exercise. Think about varying where and how you walk your dog. If you go to a nearby park and regularly drive there, why not walk to the park on days when you have more time? This will not only increase the amount of exercise that your dog is receiving, but will also

Vary the route when you take your dog out for a walk, and think about recruiting other members of the household.

bring other benefits, such as keeping your pet's nails in shape through walking on pavements.

This is also a good opportunity to improve your dog's lead-walking technique, and to remind your pet to sit at kerbs before crossing the road. Varying your walk pattern will also provide your dog with more mental stimulus. If you continue to go to a nearby park during the week, think about different routes you could take rather than using the same familiar circuit. At weekends, you can take your dog for longer walks elsewhere – not necessarily every week, but as often as possible.

Banish Boredom

Just like their human owners, dogs also suffer from boredom. This is most commonly seen in Border Collies and similar breeds, which are seen on television working in an almost intuitive way with their handlers, shepherding sheep. People often think they would make marvellous pets, but in reality, Border Collies that are left alone at home while their owners are out for much of the day, are likely to become destructive and troublesome. Many of these dogs end up on the lists of rescue organizations. The Border Collie is essentially a working breed, and will not thrive on a sedentary, isolated lifestyle, lacking any mental stimulus.

Think about getting your dog a playmate to help banish boredom.

Other dog breeds may react to boredom in a similar but less conspicuous way. In addition to destructive behaviour, they tend to overcompensate by seeking lots of attention whenever their owner is at home. Many people react by providing treats and tidbits, partly to pacify the dog, and so the ground rules that can lead to obesity become established. The dog's destructive behaviour may also have the effect of weakening the bond with its owner, who subsequently takes less interest in the dog, not playing with it or taking it out very much, which leads to the dog piling on the pounds.

Adjusting Intake

If you are feeding your dog more than is required to stay healthy, you will need to cut back on the overall food intake without causing your pet to go hungry. One of the big advantages of using a formulated weight-loss food compared with trying to devise a home-produced ration is that a good commercial diet will deliver fewer calories but has an increased fibre content to help stop the dog from feeling hungry. Weight-loss diets available on veterinary prescription may be more beneficial in treating chronic obesity, but similar foods sold in pet stores can work equally well for most dogs, again as part of a more general change in lifestyle.

It is often harder to slim down a dog using homemade foods than using a commercial weight-loss diet, because in commercial diets everything except measuring the food portion has been done for you. Homemade foods are more demanding is because it is difficult to calculate their calorie content, but there are various other simple ways of curbing your dog's intake of food. For example, switch to a low-calorie biscuit meal if you are worried about your dog's weight. In more serious cases of obesity, cut back significantly on the quantity of biscuit, which is the main source of carbohydrate in a homemade meat-based dog food, and replace this with a variety of lightly cooked vegetables, such as broccoli, carrots and beans. Drain and allow these to cool before offering them to your pet. Creating the right nutritional balance, as well as reducing calories, is a difficult problem with homemade weight-loss diets, so giving your dog vegetables will help to

Your dog should have worked up an appetite before it is fed, and will be alert and expectant at meal times.

provide valuable vitamins and minerals. Be aware that they are also likely to cause flatulence, but this may be offset to some extent by the use of garlic capsules or tablets.

Another problem with homemade diets is that they will almost inevitably require a reduction in the quantity of food when feeding a calorie-reduced diet, so your pet may now feel hungry. Adding more fibre to the diet, of low nutritional value, is therefore essential in order to help counteract this, mirroring the situation with commercially manufactured weight-loss diets.

A bored dog will inevitably turn to food as 'entertainment' especially when around family members who are also eating. It is important to provide distractions in the way of toys in such cases.

HUNGRY AND RESTLESS

Although you can cut out treats and tidbits without causing a dog to feel hungry, reducing the quantity of food in the dog's regular meals will affect its behaviour for a time. The dog is likely to be restless and reluctant to settle down, pestering you at meal times and in the kitchen – anywhere that food may be available.

Outside the home, you may find that your pet is more inclined to run off and scavenge at every opportunity, making your dog harder to control. This can be a particular problem in areas where there are other people around, perhaps having a picnic or enjoying an ice-cream in a park, because the dog is likely to bound up to them, seeking food. Remember also that such foods may make your pet ill. If you think your dog may become a nuisance in these surroundings, or you are worried about scavenging, you will need to keep your pet on a leash. If a leash is not effective on its own, a harness with a head collar can be used, or you may need to muzzle your pet when letting the dog off the lead.

Digestive Upsets

Although it is very difficult, humans can adjust to their hunger pangs when on a diet, knowing that this is serving a purpose, but dogs cannot. Their survival instincts are so strong that if they are hungry, they will seek food at every opportunity. This can lead to problems such as eating unsuitable items. Old, stale and even mouldy food will be eaten readily by a hungry dog, and this can trigger a digestive upset. It is not always easy to supervise a dog that has been let off the leash when out walking, because you will not be able to see what your pet is doing at all times. An extendible lead is invaluable in these cases.

Particularly unpleasant foods may be vomited up quite quickly, while food that is heavily contaminated by bacteria can give rise to serious diarrhoea. The situation can be worse if a dog scavenges when out walking in the countryside, where poisoned and rotten animal carcasses may be encountered.

To treat diarrhoea, keep your dog confined in a part of the home where it will be easy to clean up as necessary, and provide your pet with free access to drinking water but no food. This helps to counteract the dehydration that accompanies diarrhoea, while at the same time allowing the rhythm of the intestinal tract to settle down. Feed the dog a couple of fairly bland meals of chicken and rice afterwards, because this will be easily digested, before returning to your pet's regular type of food.

You may want to use a probiotic product with the chicken and rice. This contains beneficial bacteria that will help to restore the balance in the dog's intestinal tract. Choose an acid-fast strain if possible, because these are less likely to be destroyed in the acidic environment of the dog's stomach, before passing on to have a beneficial effect in the digestive tract. Antibiotics are not usually needed, but if the diarrhoea persists for more than 24 hours, or your dog has a chronic condition such as kidney failure that may be affected by the loss of fluid, always seek veterinary advice.

Intestinal Blockages

When out scavenging, there is also the possibility that your dog may pick up and swallow something indigestible that could lead to a blockage in the intestinal tract. Items that may be responsible include pieces of bone and food wrappers, and even less obvious things such as chunks of corn-on-the-cob or peach stones. Hide chews can also be implicated in some cases.

The resulting symptoms will depend partly on where in the intestinal tract the blockage has occurred. If the obstruction is in the duodenum, which is the first part of the small intestine immediately after the stomach, the dog is likely to vomit repeatedly and will not be able to keep food down. A blockage lower down the intestinal tract is more likely to cause constipation.

Intestinal obstructions are harder to diagnose if a dog is obese, because the vet will not be able to feel the obstruction easily. In any event, your dog is likely to need x-rays to determine the exact cause of the problem, and for the vet to see the position of the obstruction. The likelihood is that the obstruction will have to be removed surgically, which inevitably carries an increased risk if a dog is seriously overweight. In the first instance, there is the risk of anaesthetic complications, while in the longer term, the incision in the abdominal wall may not heal as readily as in a fitter individual, given the difficulty in suturing the tissue back together.

DEALING WITH AGGRESSIVENESS

The personalities of different dogs will influence the way they react to being placed on a diet. You are most likely to encounter problems with breeds such as Rottweilers and Dobermanns, or similar crosses that naturally have fairly dominant personalities. They may occasionally become aggressive and very possessive about their food. This problem is particularly likely to arise if a dog is teased with food at an early stage in life, such as having its food bowl placed in front of it and then taken away again, before being allowed to eat the food there.

In cases where a dog is aggressive and/or possessive about its food, weigh out the food carefully and then place the bowl on the ground. Do not try to add any more food after you have done this, or remove any food from the bowl, because this could serve as a potential flashpoint, leading to your being bitten. Such behaviour is not directly related to the fact that your pet is on a diet, unless the quantity of food is significantly less than normal, but the diet may aggravate bad behaviour. Dogs that behave aggressively do need treatment, whatever the cause, and it is worth discussing the problem with a canine behaviourist in order to identify the underlying reason for the behaviour and develop a strategy for overcoming it.

Abnormal Appetites

Eating disorders are not well recognized in dogs, but there are recorded cases of dogs with abnormally high appetites who will seek food constantly, although these are very rare and may have an underlying medical cause. At the other extreme, there are occasional anorexic individuals, most often among toy dogs such as Chihuahuas, although if your dog suddenly loses its appetite, the likelihood is that your pet is ill rather than anorexic.

A dog that chews plants and other items may be suffering a mineral deficiency.

Some dogs such as Beagles are naturally great scavengers, and they are among the most likely to display the condition known as pica. This causes them to eat inedible items, such as stones, or clothing such as underwear and socks left around the house. It is not an indication that they are hungry, but is thought to be a manifestation similar to obsessive-compulsive disorders seen in people. Cases tend to be most common in young dogs, and may require life-saving surgery.

One particularly unpleasant but not uncommon problem is coprophagia, when the dog eats its own faeces. The best solution is to keep temptation out of the dog's reach, clearing up thoroughly. Although the causes of this habit are unclear, it is not a sign that a dog is hungry. Such behaviour is seen especially in dogs that have spent a large part of their lives in kennels, so there may be a hygiene link. Also, bitches normally clean up their puppies' faeces until the young dogs are able to walk, as do wolves, so there may be an underlying behavioural component within the dog's psyche.

It has also been suggested that affected individuals may be deficient in B vitamins, which can be synthesized by bacteria in the lower part of the digestive tract, although they cannot be absorbed there and so pass out of the body. This can be remedied by adding naturally rich sources of these vitamins, such as brewers' yeast tablets or powder, to the food. Dogs will sometimes seek out the droppings of herbivores such as sheep or deer when out for a walk and consume these, probably for a similar reason, again, not due to hunger.

Family Problems

If you are to address the problem of your dog's obesity, you will need to seek the co-operation of all the other members of the household, younger ones in particular. There is little to be gained by you enforcing a rigorous ban on treats if the children still feed the family pet with tidbits at every meal. It can sometimes be hard to persuade them to stop, because they will often regard it as cruel to the dog.

There is also likely to be the associated problem, particularly when children have friends visiting, that uneaten food will be left temptingly within reach of your pet. Items such as abandoned slices of pizza provide a significant hike in your dog's daily calorific intake, with a burger typically having enough calories to meet a medium-sized dog's entire energy needs for two days. Clearly, this can easily ruin your best endeavours when trying to slim down your pet.

You therefore need to talk to your children at the outset and explain the situation to them in terms that they will understand. Make sure they know why they must not feed the dog tidbits, or leave food where a pet can steal it easily. It often helps if you get the children involved in the weight-loss plan. Encourage them to measure out your pet's food and help in the weighing process, to enable them to see the benefits themselves.

This can also be a good opportunity to encourage the children to play with the dog more, and while their keen level of interest may only be maintained for a short period of time, compared with that needed to get your pet back to its target weight, it can still make a real difference.

Many children see feeding their dog as entertainment, because it is a quick way of getting a dog's attention. It is important children know the harm they may be doing by overfeeding their pet.

Dog Walkers and Dog Sitters

It is not uncommon for a change in an owner's life, such as greater family commitments or a new job, to reduce the amount of time they have available to exercise their dog. While placing a dog on a diet is easy compared with increasing the level of exercise, the latter is vital in helping the dog to lose weight and improve its overall level of fitness. If it is difficult to exercise your dog regularly yourself, you could employ a dog-walking agency.

Businesses of this type are well established in many areas, and can be a real help if you find yourself short of time. The walkers generally take out more than one dog at a time, however, so your pet is unlikely to be allowed to run for long off the leash, if at all. This can be a drawback, but on the other hand, interaction with other dogs while out walking will help to use up more energy.

Even if you have the time to take your dog out for a walk each day, you could use a dog-walking service to boost the amount of exercise your dog is receiving by giving your pet a second walk every day. Some agencies also provide dog-sitting services. They will collect your pet in the morning, look after it during the day, including providing exercise, and then bring your pet home later. This can also help as part of a weight-loss programme if you are out at work during the day, when your dog is likely to spend most of its time asleep. Your pet is likely to be far more active and less bored at a dog sitter's, where there is someone around all day and other dogs to play with.

You will need to find out about feeding arrangements and explain that your dog is on a strict weight-loss diet. Ideally, you should remain in charge of feeding your pet, so you can be certain about the quantity of food. Stress to the dog sitter that it is very important that your dog has nothing to eat while away from home, other than any food that you provide.

QUESTIONS TO ASK DOG WALKERS

- How long have they being doing this professionally?
- What experience do they have of dogs?
- Do they have references available?
- Do they have insurance cover?

- Would your dog be walked on its own or with a group of other dogs?
- If as part of a group, how many dogs do they take out at a time ?
- Where do they take the dogs?

Exercise Plans

There is no standard type of exercise plan that is suitable for all dogs, because of the differences in their anatomy as well as their natural level of activity. An athletic Labrador Retriever can be put through a much wider and more demanding range of exercise routines than an ambling Bulldog or a Dachshund with a history of spinal disc problems.

Your dog will also give clear indications of its own tolerance levels for exercise. The idea is to boost your dog's natural level of activity when out walking, building up fitness levels as well as lowering weight. Once a dog feels that it has walked far enough, the likelihood is that the dog will start to lag behind, pausing frequently. This is the time to turn around and head back home.

You should then find that your dog settles down readily and sleeps for a period. On the other hand, if your dog remains lively after you arrive home, the likelihood is that the walk was too short.

The weather may also play a part in your dog's enthusiasm for exercise. Short- and thin-coated breeds, such as the Italian Greyhound, are likely to be unenthusiastic about walking when it is cold and wet. Conversely, long-coated breeds like the Pyrenean Mountain Dog will probably have less energy when the weather is hot. It is particularly important to be guided by an overweight dog's reaction to exercise in order to avoid problems such as lameness and the associated pain that is a symptom of various joint ailments.

NO QUICK FIXES

Beware of any methods promoting weight loss with minimal input on your part. Do not, for example, fix a metal peg in the lawn and attach your dog to this, allowing him to roam around the area alone. Your dog is at serious risk from the elements in these surroundings even if a kennel is nearby. A dog could succumb to heat stroke if it tips over or empties the water bowl on a hot day, and

it is unlikely the dog will take any more exercise if kept outdoors in this way than it would inside the home. There are other associated health risks, such as skin cancer, which tends to affect the ears. Many dogs become frustrated when tethered, which causes them to bark incessantly, giving rise to complaints from neighbours as well as the risk of your pet developing laryngitis.

Implementing the Plan

If you are to implement a weight-loss plan successfully, there are a number of things to bear in mind. For example, it is important to convince your dog that it is not losing out on food, despite being on a diet. Here, you can put some canine psychology to good use. One of the best strategies is to divide the daily ration of food into several smaller feeds during the course of the day, rather than just offering a single meal as you may have done in the past. By interspersing this with plenty of activity, such as walks and games, you will distract your dog from thinking about food as the central focus of its day. This will help to cure your pet of eating out of boredom as well as strengthen the bond between you.

As you slim down your dog, your relationship with your pet will change as a result. For example, if you have stopped giving out treats on demand, you will find that you subsequently take more notice of your dog, rewarding your pet with praise rather than food, and thereby reinforcing the relationship between you.

Read the Labels

If you use a commercially prepared weight-loss diet for your dog, it will provide clear guidance on the quantity of food required for the size of dog. Remember that a larger dog needs proportionately fewer calories per pound or kilogram compared with a toy breed. As a result, a Great Dane requires only about 20 calories per pound, compared with a Chihuahua that needs 60 calories. This difference is due to their level of activity as well as the fact that a Chihuahua requires more energy to maintain its body temperature because of its small size.

Calculate the number of calories that your pet is currently receiving, bearing in mind that a dry diet contains roughly three times more calories than the same sized portion of wet food (see also page 46). You can reduce an overweight dog's food intake by about 20 per cent in order to effect the required loss in weight if you switch to a formulated weight-loss diet.

Once the dog has reached its target weight, do not rush to increase the amount of food that you are offering, but instead monitor your dog's progress. If necessary, increase the amount of food slightly, especially if the dog has become more active, but be sure not to offer any treats or tidbits that will lead to an increase in weight beyond what is healthy.

Size and your dog's level of activity are two factors influencing its nutritional needs.

The situation will be more complicated if you are using home-cooked food, especially if you vary the diet significantly, because it is much harder to calculate calorie intake and adjust it accordingly. With wrapped food, such as rice and supermarket meat, you are likely to find the calorific details on the packaging, so when you weigh out how much

food to give your pet, use this information to calculate the number of calories.

At this point, it will be worthwhile trying to standardize the type of fresh food that you are offering, so that you can assess the calories more easily. It is equally important not to give your pet any leftover table scraps in addition to this food. If you want to carry on offering food of this type, along with treats, you must allow for these in the overall daily calorie allowance.

Keep a Diary

Get a diary and use it to record your dog's weight on the first day of the diet. Weigh your dog first thing in the morning, before feeding, to obtain an accurate indication of weight, then continue to do so weekly. A weekend may be the best time to do this, when things are generally less busy.

If your dog is pure-bred, you can find the target weight from the breed standard (see page 141). Subtract this figure from your dog's present weight to determine how much needs to be lost, then calculate a weekly weight-loss schedule to take your dog down to this ideal figure. A dog should not lose more than 2 per cent of its body weight each week, with 1.5 per cent often being recommended for older dogs. This means that the amount of weight that should be lost will reduce slightly as the weeks pass. Using the 2 per cent guideline as an example, if a dog currently weighs 100lb (45.36 kg) and has a target weight of 80 lb (36.29 kg), in the first week it should lose 2 lb (0.9 kg), taking the dog down to 98 lb (44.45 kg). During the second week, the dog's weight should fall by 2 per cent of 98lb (44.45 kg), which is 1.96 lb (0.88 kg). You can work this out easily using a calculator. Write in the diary what the target weight should be for each week, and refer to this to check on your pet's progress. In this particular case, it would take about 11 weeks to get the dog down to the target weight. In reality, it may take some dogs slightly longer to reach the target weight, but the main thing is that your pet is shedding the pounds progressively.

Extra Food Sources

Obviously, it is important to check your dog's weight does not start to creep up again at any stage. If it does, you need to find the cause, and remedy it. It may be that, unknown to you, another member of the family has mistakenly fed the dog on several occasions when you were out, thinking that you had not done so before you left. There is also the possibility that your dog may

If you have placed your dog on a diet but it fails to lose weight, make sure younger family members are not giving it extra treats or table scraps without your knowledge.

have been receiving food from other sources, such as younger members of the family, who might buy a burger and fries in the park and share a little of this calorie-laden food with the dog, thinking that this treat would cause no harm.

There is also the possibility that your dog may be stealing food elsewhere. Many dogs take a keen interest in what is placed on bird tables in the garden, and larger individuals may even be able to stand up on their hindlegs and help themselves, being particularly inclined to do so if there are household foods such as bread or bacon rinds there. Dogs tend not to eat bird seed itself, with the exception of peanuts.

Take particular care if you are hanging up fat balls in the garden, because these often prove irresistible to dogs in spite of the seeds stuck in the suet. Always tie this type of food securely around a branch where it will not be easily dislodged, even in windy weather, ensuring that it will remain out of reach of your pet. Do not tie it to a bird table, because a large dog may be able to knock this over and so reach the fat ball, with the thin nylon mesh often fitted around such products presenting no barrier to your dog's teeth.

Rubbish bags can also provide a dog with additional food, so you need to be certain that these are not left lying about outside where your dog can rip them apart in search of edible items. If you notice that your dog appears to be spending longer outside in the garden than usual, do not assume this is because of newfound energy and fitness arising as a result of a diet. Instead, this is much more likely to indicate that your pet has found a way into a neighbour's property, or may even be roaming the streets, eating scraps of food, and then returning home in due course.

It is a good idea to check your boundary fencing regularly, to ensure that your dog has not been digging under it, or that the wind has not weakened the fencing and created a gap large enough for your dog to squeeze through. Dogs can be surprisingly agile if they are keen to get under a fence, being able to flatten themselves on to all fours, while they can also jump well.

Straying unbeknown to you carries an additional risk, which may explain not just a failure to lose weight but also unexpected weight gain if your pet is an unspayed bitch. She may have slipped out while in heat, mated and become pregnant. Do not assume that your dog is simply hungry if she tries to disappear; bitches may actively seek a mate when in heat.

Home Danger

Your dog may not be able to resist stealing your food if an opportunity presents itself, although it is less likely to do this while you are present. Do not leave temptation available. When you come in after shopping, avoid leaving bags containing food within easy reach of your pet, because this will encourage your dog to steal when your attention is distracted elsewhere. Not only could this have an adverse effect on your dog's diet, but it could also have more serious consequences if your pet eats something that disagrees with it.

Chocolate, in particular, is very appealing to dogs, but can prove deadly to them because it contains theobromine and caffeine. Both these ingredients can have serious effects on the heart and respiratory system, causing death, while the high fat content of chocolate can lead to inflammation of the pancreas as well. Dark chocolate contains much higher levels of theobromine than milk chocolate. Small dogs may be more at risk than their larger relatives because of the size of chocolate bars; they need to eat proportionately less to be affected. In some cases, the ingesting of chocolate can be fatal, so be especially concerned if your dog does not vomit up the chocolate bar soon after swallowing because the active ingredients will be absorbed into the bloodstream.

Various other items of shopping can also be harmful. Macadamia nuts are dangerous for dogs, resulting in vomiting, weakness and

MULTI-PET HOUSEHOLDS

An overweight dog may steal food from other household pets if given the chance. Dogs will readily steal cat food, so you may have to develop a separate feeding routine, feeding them in different rooms, if you have a cat. Cats tend to be fussier eaters than dogs, and may not eat their entire ration immediately that it is provided. Try encouraging your cat to feed by putting down the food bowl and then taking it away again, repeating this at several stages through the day.

The same applies if you have two dogs and are trying to slim down one of them. The dieting dog may try to steal some of its companion's food, so feed them separately. This is an easier scenario than when a cat is involved, because both dogs will eat their food rapidly.

If you have other pets in your household, do not leave their food where a dieting dog could steal it.

DANGERS IN THE KITCHEN

Keep your dog outside the room when cooking in the kitchen. Your pet would be at serious risk of an accident, or of getting burned on the hob, if he stood on his hindlegs and tried to reach food on the work surface.

Some foods can be dangerous while they are being prepared, and this does not just mean raw meat. Make sure you exclude your dog from the kitchen if you are making bread, for example. If your pet manages to steal and eat raw bread dough, this is likely to swell up in the stomach and can easily create a serious, life-threatening obstruction. In addition, the yeast in the dough produces alcohol in the form of ethanol, which will be absorbed into the bloodstream, causing drunkenness that may also prove fatal, depending on the quantity absorbed.

Below is a list of items that are harmful to dogs, so make sure these are kept out of reach of scavenging pets:

• Apple pips
• Avocado
• Alcohol and products containing alcohol
• Cannabis
• Chocolate
• Coffee beans and grounds
• Dough
• Grapes and raisins
• Onions
• Stones of fruits such as plums and apricots
• Tobacco

unsteadiness on the feet, but the effects are transitory. Raisins on their own or in cakes can have a much more serious impact on your dog's health, triggering kidney failure, as will grapes. Unfortunately, just as with chocolate, your dog will not appreciate the danger and will eat this fruit readily. You may not be aware of any problem for several hours, until the dog suddenly starts to appear very ill, suffering from vomiting and diarrhoea. The actual reason that raisins and grapes cause this reaction is unclear at present, although raisins are more deadly than grapes because they contain a much lower percentage of water after being dried.

Avocado has also been documented as being harmful to dogs, so do not leave either the fruit, or even the large seeds in a location where your dog could steal them. The active ingredient in the avocado is persin, which will damage the dog's heart muscle. It seems that the effects are likely to be worse with Guatemalan strains of this fruit.

Going for Walks

Perhaps unsurprisingly, slimming down a dog can prove easier in the summer months if you live in a temperate climate, although this is not an excuse to delay placing your dog on a diet during the winter. In summer, when the weather is warm, you are more likely to take your dog out for longer walks, than on a bitterly cold day, and the dog is also likely to be more enthusiastic about playing outdoors when the weather is good.

The way in which you increase your dog's exercise to achieve weight loss and increased fitness, will to some extent depend on the dog's age, and its overall state of health. Changes do not need to be dramatic. Look for more opportunities to take out your dog, even if it is only for short walks, because this is a valuable way of giving your pet more exercise and helping to build up its fitness.

Take time to think about how you are going to give your pet more exercise. Decide on a plan that works for you; ultimately, it may mean a change of lifestyle.

Unfortunately, this is not always easy. If you are going to the shops, for example, you may not be able to take your dog into the store with you, and often there is nowhere to leave a dog tied up outside. There is also the risk of dog-napping if you do leave your pet tied to a pole. Some dogs have been taken from outside shops and similar localities by the unscrupulous, with their distraught owners then being asked to pay a ransom to have their pet returned to them (it is not just valuable pure-bred dogs that are targeted; any dog is potentially at risk). If you are going to the shops, therefore, try to persuade another member of the family to go with you, so that your dog does not have to be left alone at any stage.

Of course, taking your dog with you to the shops or to post a letter is not a substitute for a main walk. If you usually only take your dog out for a proper walk once a day, try to double up so that your pet is exercised both morning and evening. Gradually increase the length of the walks, and see how your dog reacts. If your pet shows signs of tiredness, stop and head back home.

Ball Games

If taking your dog out for more walks is not feasible, there are alternative methods you can employ inside the home and garden to improve your pet's fitness. For example, you can encourage your dog to run up and down the hall in your home chasing a ball, assuming this is largely free of furniture or valuable objects that could be knocked over and broken or even hurt the dog.

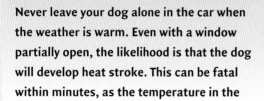

DRIVING DANGERS

Never leave your dog alone in the car when the weather is warm. Even with a window partially open, the likelihood is that the dog will develop heat stroke. This can be fatal within minutes, as the temperature in the vehicle, which is effectively a metal box, rises dramatically. Sadly, dogs do die in this way every year, with obese, short-faced breeds such as boxers being especially vulnerable. If in doubt, leave your dog at home.

Dogs instinctively tend to pursue a ball, even if they have not done so before, and particularly when playing with you on a one-to-one basis. You then simply need to call the dog back to you. Your dog will soon learn to drop the ball so that you can roll it along the floor again. If your pet has not learned this command, you may need to open its jaws slightly to remove the ball.

If you have to open the dog's mouth, place your left hand across the bridge of the nose to steady the upper jaw (assuming that you are right-handed), and then prise down the lower jaw slightly with your other hand, which will be sufficient to persuade the dog to drop the ball or indeed any other toy. Before long, you are likely to find that the dog not only drops the ball at your feet, but also seeks you out with a ball in its mouth, hoping that you will play along. Games of this type – whether indoors or out – help to improve a dog's agility, co-ordination and mental fitness, as well as burning off calories.

Playing with a ball is something that is best encouraged from the time a dog is a puppy. It will promote fitness and ultimately a healthy pet.

You may well find that your dog starts to play ball games alone. If your garden is on a slope, the dog may take a ball out and chase it down the incline. Indoors, your pet may sit at the top of the stairs and let the ball start rolling down, before running down to the bottom to pick it up again.

This type of exercise can be beneficial in terms of aiding weight loss and improving your pet's fitness, although smaller breeds such as Dachshunds that are susceptible to slipped discs should not be encouraged to play on the stairs because they could injure themselves.

Tug Toys and Chews

Some dogs enjoy playing with tug toys and chews. However, these toys can encourage dogs to play too vigorously if unchecked, particularly tug toys that the dog tries to pull out of your grasp. Tug toys appeal to powerful breeds such as Bull Terriers and Rottweilers, and can use up a lot of energy on the dog's part, but you need to ensure that the game does not become too violent.

Certain chews can be used in a similar way to tug toys, and can keep a dog occupied when left on its own, helping to prevent boredom. They are good for dogs that are naturally inclined to be destructive, because they serve to divert their attention from other potential targets in the home, such as a chair or table leg.

Chewing household objects like shoes is a common sign of boredom, particularly once a dog is over six months old and has finished teething. Regard this as a warning sign in a young dog, because boredom is an underlying factor that has been implicated in obesity. Dogs will eat more if they have nothing else to do, so anything that

POSSESSIVENESS TOWARDS TOYS

Dogs can become possessive towards their toys, especially bitches suffering from a false pregnancy, which cause them to behave as if the toys were her puppies. If your dog reacts aggressively when a toy is taken away – essentially the reaction of an animal that feels insecure – you may need to speak with your vet about dealing with this behaviour.

enlivens their day is to be recommended. Toys help to take their mind off food, just as the excitement of going out for a walk does.

Although chew toys are relatively robust, most are likely to be destroyed eventually. A simple, colourful chew toy may therefore be a better option than an expensive one. Match the size of the toy to that of your dog, so that your pet can carry the toy and play with it easily. Lightweight chew toys can also be used in chase-and-retrieve games. These are much easier to play with well-trained dogs, but this may not be the case if you have taken on a rescue dog. You will need to encourage your dog to drop the toy readily if you are to be able to play in this way. Most dogs will quickly learn this command, but initially you may

Make sure that you 'win' at tug-of-war most of the time. This will help to prevent your dog from developing a possessive streak towards its toys.

have to prise the toy out of your pet's mouth in the same way as you would a ball (see page 115).

There is no need to give your dog a large number of toys to chew; two or three is more than sufficient as long as they are of a safe design. Unfortunately, there are no real standards in this area, partly because dogs differ significantly in how destructive they are towards toys. Beware of rope chew toys, for example, if you think that your dog is destroying these and might be swallowing the fibres. Solid chews may be better in this case.

GIVE A DOG A BONE?

Do not be tempted to give your dog bones unless they are large marrowbones. These are relatively safe, although if used exclusively they can cause excessive wear on the teeth. Any bones from chicken carcasses are exceedingly dangerous, because they may splinter and stick in the throat if swallowed, causing your dog to choke. Never give a joint of meat that is on the bone to your dog.

The major drawback of using bones to occupy your dog rather than a toy is that they are not hygienic in the home; they are likely to attract flies, especially in summer.

It may be a good idea to restrict your dog to having a bone in the garden only, although there is the risk that the bone will be taken by other animals such as foxes.

Other Toys and Games

The many different toys now available can all be valuable when encouraging a dog to take more exercise. It is worthwhile visiting a pet store where there is a good selection of toys so that you can find something that your dog likes. Some dogs prefer simple toys such as dumbbells that they can carry around with them, and that make a squeaky noise when they are picked up. When you give your dog a new toy, do not simply drop it in front of your pet; instead, demonstrate how to play with it for a few moments. Just like a child with a new toy, most dogs appear to prefer their latest toy at first, but within a few days you will notice that old favourites re-emerge and start to be played with more frequently again.

Some toys have a very unpredictable bounce, especially when thrown on to a hard surface, and your dog is likely to enjoy playing with one of these as an alternative to a ball. The dog has to anticipate how the toy will bounce in order to have any hope of catching it. You can take these toys with you when out on a walk with your pet, provided you are going to an area of open grassland where the toy will not get lost. Toys of this type can be purchased in a variety of sizes, making them suitable for all dogs.

Whereas balls and similar toys can be used anywhere, flying discs require lots of space, encouraging dogs to run farther afield. When walking your dog with someone else, throw the disc from one person to the other; your dog will run up and down, trying to intercept the disc. Allow the dog to catch the disc on occasion so that your pet does not become frustrated by the game and lose interest. Reward the dog's success by throwing the disc several times for your pet to chase after on its own, before repeating the game with your companion.

There are also toys that can help to keep your pet active in your absence. These can take the form of a hollow toy with a cut in one side that your dog has to manipulate in order to extract food, such as a piece of carrot. This type of activity is recommended for older dogs that need to lose weight, because it promotes activity without straining aging joints. It also helps to encourage mental alertness, and can therefore help to offset canine cognitive dysfunction, sometimes described as canine Alzheimer's disease. This particular illness is becoming increasingly common today because dogs are living longer now than in the past.

You can also play hide-and-seek with your dog, both in the home and outside. This will stimulate mental alertness as well as increase the amount of exercise your pet is getting. Start by teaching this game to your dog at home, then begin playing it when you are out on a walk. When your dog is off the leash, dart behind a tree for example, and call your pet's name. Your dog should then come bounding over to find you, after which remember to lavish your pet with praise.

A number of toys that are available commercially are specially designed to bounce in a 'random' way.

Another Dog?

You may be tempted to get a second dog so that your pets can keep each other occupied when you are out or busy. While this will have the desired effect, the fact is that if you do not have enough time for one dog, you will not have time for a second one. Both dogs will still require time and attention from you, and the cost of food, veterinary services and kennelling will double.

If you decide that you do have the time, energy and resources for a second dog, bear in mind the following: dogs, like people, have highly individual and largely unaccountable likes and dislikes when it comes to choosing playmates. There is no real evidence that dogs of particular

Although it is not necessary to get a second dog of the same breed as your first pet, it is a good idea to get one that has the same natural level of activity so that they can run around together at the same pace.

CANINE COUCH POTATOES

While playing games will improve your dog's co-ordination, muscular tone and fitness, they will also keep your pet mentally alert. If your pet is something of a couch potato and enjoys watching television, however, you can leave this on occasionally when you go out. There are even special DVDs available for dogs to watch, which sighthounds in particular often find fascinating. Try these when you are at home first, to test your dog's reaction. Some dogs also appear to enjoy listening to the radio. While these pastimes will not exercise your dog, they will amuse your pet when you go out and provide mental stimulation.

breeds seek out similar companions, so you need not feel obliged to acquire another dog of the same breed if your existing pet is pure-bred. It is not unusual for a smaller dog to play with a larger one, and often the smaller dog will prove to be the dominant individual. However, certain breeds are more well disposed to others of their own kind for obvious reasons. For example, a sighthound may prefer to play with another sighthound because they can run together quickly. When obtaining a second dog to help keep a dog's

weight down, think about acquiring an active dog, in the hope that it will help to keep your existing dog fit. Breeds with dog fighting in their ancestry, such as Bull Terriers, are less likely to be sociable with other dogs, whether of their own or a different breed.

It is worth observing how your dog behaves with other dogs when out for a walk. This may help you to reach a decision about acquiring another pet, and what type of dog may be most appropriate. If you do decide to get a second dog, it is usually

EXTENDIBLE LEASHES

If you are worried about your new dog's reaction to being off the leash, and whether he will return readily, you can buy an extendible leash to use until you are sure he will return of his own accord. This allows the dog freedom to roam over a wider area than when on a conventional leash, and allows you to retract it and keep your dog closer to you when necessary, such as when crossing a road.

This type of leash is most suitable in open areas with no trees or bushes in which the leash can become entangled. They can also be useful in an urban location, such as alongside a canal or similar stretch of water where it may not be safe to allow the dog off the leash. Just as with ordinary leashes, the extendible kind are made in different styles, catering for dogs of all sizes.

not too difficult to introduce a companion to your existing pet because dogs are social by nature. Introduce them on neutral territory if possible, by taking them for a walk together. You should go with someone else and you should take one dog each. Put them on extendible leashes and gradually allow them to get nearer to each other, while you and your companion remain at a distance from both. This is definitely the best approach if you are thinking of acquiring a rescued dog, which may be nervous around other dogs. You can then gauge how both dogs get along, before making a firm commitment.

Certain introductions are easier to oversee than others, largely reflecting the respective social status of the dogs themselves, irrespective of their origins. Two male dogs are less likely to get along than two bitches or neutered individuals. It is also often easier to introduce a young dog to an older companion. This is the ideal combination for improving the older dog's fitness, and a middle-aged dog in particular can benefit from this situation.

One of the keys to ensuring a harmonious introduction is not to undermine the position of your existing pet in the family hierarchy. Although your natural instinct will be to pay more attention to the newcomer, this will be counterproductive. You need to reinforce your existing pet's social status, so that the newcomer will not challenge this. Always pay greater attention to your existing dog, allowing the newcomer to establish a separate role.

Feeding can be a particular area of conflict. It is important to feed the dogs separately, preferably at different times. What you definitely do not want is for your established pet to start stealing the food of the newcomer, undermining all that you have done in bringing down its weight. Keeping them apart will also prevent any risk of aggression at this stage.

When they are out and off the leash, the likelihood is that the dogs will run along together, reinforcing the bond that they have built up at home, giving both of them more exercise than if you took them out individually. Even so, you need to be sure that both respond well to your instructions, especially if you are in areas where there could be farmstock. Bear in mind that a puppy cannot be let off the leash until it has mastered basic training and will return to you without hesitation when called, which will take several months. If you are keen to acquire a new dog that will encourage your existing pet to exercise more, it should be easier and quicker to work with a dog that has already been trained.

PARKS AND GYMS

If you decide not to get a second dog, you may be able to take your pet to a special dog park. Popular in North America, these are confined areas where dogs can play together – great if your dog is not especially nervous. It is important to ensure your pet's vaccinations are current, as the likelihood of infections spreading is higher in areas where dogs congregate together. Similarly flea treatments can stop you bringing these parasites home with you. There are also pet gyms in some areas, with special treadmills and similar equipment where your dog can be exercised safely.

Preventing a Relapse

Although it will be a great moment when your dog reaches its target weight, bear in mind that this is really only the beginning. Hopefully the whole experience of slimming down your dog will have brought you closer together, but you need to check that your pet does not regain any of those lost pounds.

The increased range of activities that you have undertaken as part of this campaign should be continued in order to maintain your dog's weight and build up its level of fitness. However, once your dog is fit, you may like to expand its exercise routine to include more strenuous activities such as those described in this chapter.

Hiking

There is a surprisingly wide range of activities that can be undertaken with dogs, and a number of these replicate, at least in part, the original purpose for which the dog was bred. Scenthounds such as Beagles are bred to cover large distances at a steady pace, so an ideal way of exercising them once they are fit is to go on long-distance hikes. Do not forget to take drinking water for your pet, especially in warm weather. Other dogs that can benefit from this type of exercise are various gundogs, including Labrador Retrievers and Spaniels, that naturally work for long periods in the field.

Just like at the start of the weight-loss programme, you need to continue the process of improving your dog's fitness by gradually increasing the distances of walks over a period of time. Do not suddenly set off on a marathon hike, but instead build up to gradually longer walks over successive weeks.

Mountain Biking

While scenthounds tend to display great stamina, sighthounds prefer to run quickly over shorter distances, and this is where mountain biking in the countryside may be a good way of maintaining your dog's fitness. The problem with riding a bike elsewhere is that your dog could end up being injured or running into traffic, so it really is best to be right out in the countryside.

HEALTH CHECK

Before embarking on any of the more strenuous activities described in this chapter, arrange for your dog to be given a check by a veterinarian if you are in any doubt about your pet's health. For example, avoid exercises such as hiking if you suspect your dog has an underlying medical problem such as hip dysplasia, which will make walking painful; always suspect this if a dog is lame on waking up in the morning. The cause is a weakness in the hip joints.

A dog will soon learn to trot alongside you if you start biking, but avoid over-tiring your pet, particularly in the case of older dogs.

Even in the countryside, avoid areas where there may be livestock that could distract your dog. The best way to start, therefore, is to check out the route beforehand, to ensure that it will be safe for you and your dog. Be particularly careful if the path you are on narrows significantly at any stage, because you will need to slow down to avoid the risk of injuring your dog if it runs alongside you.

It is sometimes recommended to attach the dog's leash to part of the bike, but this can be dangerous to both of you. If you ride over an obstruction on the route, such as a raised tree root, you may end up being thrown off, injuring your dog as well; if your dog tries to run ahead while attached to the bike, this could also cause trouble. In addition, there is the risk that the leash may become caught up in the wheels or gears of the bike. Always wear a cycling helmet and take a mobile phone with you so that you can summon help if you do have an accident.

If the dog is tied to the bike by a leash, the dog will have to run at the same speed as the bike. Smaller dogs in particular are unlikely to be able to keep up, and this may also lead to considerable wear and tear on your pet's joints. Dogs soon learn to run alongside a bike without being attached by a leash, so train your dog to behave in this way; this is the safer option because there will be no direct link between you. You can also adjust your speed easily, to allow your dog to keep up. With a toy dog, you may even be able to cycle home with your pet confined in a suitable carrier attached to the bike.

What you will need to ensure, however, is that your dog does not race alongside other bikes when out for an ordinary walk; this could surprise and distract the bike riders, possibly causing them to crash. You could be legally liable if your dog causes an accident, so it is essential to have third party liability insurance cover for your pet. This may be incorporated into a standard pet insurance policy, or can be an option under some household insurance policies.

Jogging

Another form of exercise that you and your dog can engage in together is jogging, though you should not do so until your dog is fit and back at its target weight. Even then, you will need to build up the distance that you run together gradually. It is also important that the weather conditions are suitable, because dogs should not exercise in this way if it is very cold or hot.

If your dog is elderly or has a serious heart problem, this type of exercise is likely to be too vigorous. Nor is jogging suitable for small dogs, because their stride length is such that they will not be able to keep up with you. Jogging is most suitable for dogs that regularly travel quite fast over relatively long distances and have plenty of stamina. These include sled dog breeds such as the Samoyed, for example.

Jogging can be an ideal way of keeping both you and your dog fit, as well as providing a great opportunity to explore the countryside.

Cani-Cross Competitions

Increased interest in competitive racing as a way for people to keep fit has now spilled over into the canine field, with the development of cani-cross racing. This first began in North America and northern Europe as a way of keeping sled dogs fit. Dog and owner running a course of about 3.3 miles (5.4 km) are likely to cover this distance in about 20 minutes together, depending on local conditions.

The dogs are fitted with special harnesses that wrap around their bodies, rather than racing on normal collars and leashes, which would be harmful. The leash attaches to the harness near the base of the tail, so that the dog's power stems

A run through the woods is a great way to keep fit and maintain your interest as well as that of your dog.

SKIJORING AND GRASSJORING

A North American variation of cani-cross known as skijoring involves a team of as many as three dogs pulling a person along on a snowboard or skis. An alternative in the summer months is grassjoring, over grassy areas. A quick-release hook is an essential part of the equipment, so that you can separate the dogs from you to avoid an accident. The powerful Spitz breeds that originate from the far north are most suited to this type of activity. The person is not simply a dead weight being pulled along by the dogs, however, but actually snowboards or skis at the same time.

from its chest, rather than putting pressure on the neck. The human runner is connected to the dog by means of a special belt, allowing him or her to run more effectively with hands free. Never be tempted to try this type of exercise without the proper equipment, because you can easily injure your dog as a consequence. If you have difficulty finding the equipment locally, track down mail-order suppliers on the internet.

When you start out, only go with one dog, although experienced cani-cross runners may take two dogs with them, using a special neckline to keep the dogs together and ensure that they run as a team. It usually helps if the dogs are a sled breed, being instinctively used to working as a team, but at many events of this type any dogs with good stamina can take part, including Labrador Retrievers and Staffordshire Bull Terriers. Cani-cross is regarded as a winter sport in countries such as the UK, where racing in the summer could leave the dogs at risk of heat stroke, but tends to be carried out in the summer in northerly areas where the weather is cooler.

The rules vary according to the event: in some cases, all the entrants start off together; in others, they race individually, with their starting and finishing times being noted to find the pair that completes the course in the quickest time. Do not forget to have drinking water and a bowl with you.

If you like the sound of cani-cross but you do not wish to compete, you can try your hand at this type of exercise by simply running through trails in the woods. Take a stopwatch with you so that you can monitor your time, competing against your personal best rather than other runners. It is surprising how the dog's energy can help to propel you along much quicker than if you were running on your own. Even at its most basic, cani-cross can be fun and will help to keep both you and your dog fit.

Taking a Dip

Swimming is an ideal exercise for elderly dogs that may no longer be able to walk long distances because of musculo-skeletal problems. Even once your dog has slimmed down, regular visits to a hydrotherapy pool will continue to be beneficial. You may also want to allow your dog to swim in areas that you know are safe when you are out walking, but only encourage this on warm days. It is a good idea to pack a towel, to rub down your dog afterwards, so there is no risk of catching a chill, but the coats of most dogs dry remarkably quickly. They will shake themselves vigorously when they emerge from the water, and this removes much of the water from the coat, even in the case of those breeds that have dense undercoats. Thin-coated dogs are at greater risk of becoming chilled, but even they dry off very quickly on a warm day.

Avoid allowing your dog to swim every day, however, even where it is suitable to do so, because this strips vital oils out of the coat, causing both the fur and the underlying coat to become dry. Having to shampoo your dog, to remove salt from the coat if your pet has been in the sea for example, will exacerbate this situation.

Retrievers love retrieving and will readily swim out to fetch a stick or floating ball. They have been known to swim long distances.

AFTER EXERCISING

If your dog is simply muddy after exercise, it is better to allow the mud to dry, which it usually does very quickly, so that you can just brush this out of the coat, rather than having to bathe him. This may be unavoidable though, if he has plunged into dirty water or has been in the sea. Otherwise, most dogs only need to be bathed every six to eight weeks on average. There are special canine shampoos available that are used in the same way as ordinary shampoo. When bathing your pet, it is a good idea to use a plastic bath of a suitable size, such as that used for a baby, that you can place outside and partially fill with tepid water. You will also need a container, such as a jug or a clean, empty plastic ice-cream tub.

You will then need to lift the dog into the bath, but take care when doing so because your pet is likely to start struggling. Use the container to bale water over the dog's hindquarters, moving forward up to the base of the neck. You should then gently rub the shampoo into the coat, working the suds down around the underside of the body. The vast majority of dogs dislike having their head washed, so do this very carefully at the end, and ensure that no shampoo enters the eyes, where it is likely to sting.

Allow the dog to step out of the bath, standing back if you want to avoid getting wet because the dog will shake itself vigorously to remove water from its coat. Keep your pet tied up nearby on a leash while you empty the bath and rinse out any residual traces of shampoo. Partially refill the bath with tepid water, lift your dog back in, then rinse any remaining traces of shampoo out of its coat. Allow the dog to step out of the bath and shake itself again.

After bathing, do not to take your dog for a walk in areas of the countryside where your pet is likely to encounter cow pats. Bathing not only cleans the coat, but also removes the characteristic doggy odour that is an integral part of the dog's standing in canine society. Rather than waiting for this characteristic odour to return, your dog is likely to develop a new, more pungent scent by rolling in cow manure, which will necessitate another bath.

Agility Competitions

Although some of the aforementioned activities are not suitable for small dogs, there is no reason why they cannot take part in agility competitions as a way of maintaining their fitness. These have become popular with owners of dogs of all shapes and sizes, with both pure-bred and non-pedigree dogs taking part. You can attend special agility training sessions with your pet, details of which you may be able to obtain from your vet's surgery, in the advertisement columns of your local newspaper or on the internet.

These competitions are exciting to watch, and are a popular feature of many dog shows. Agility competitions test not just fitness, but also co-ordination and reaction times, with the bond between dog and handler being a vital component in such events. Agility courses differ in their

Dogs can be taught to jump through hoops, but watch out as they can jump fences that are the same height!

designs, but they usually incorporate elements such as tunnels that your dog needs to scramble through, as well as poles to weave around and obstacles to jump and climb, with each contestant taking part against the clock. The dog that makes the fewest mistakes and completes the course in the shortest time is the winner, with the handler running alongside the dog on the course, communicating what is required by a series of verbal and hand signals, as well as giving plenty of vocal encouragement. Actually touching the dog or steering it with your hands in the right direction, however, is against the rules.

Another advantage of agility contests is that they encourage dogs to socialize with each other, although each completes the course singly rather than in pairs, even when there is an opposing team. Medium-sized dogs tend to come out on top in agility competitions, rather than larger, heavier dogs such as Rottweilers. Perhaps unsurprisingly, this is often an area where Collies do well, thanks to their intelligence and the way in which they seem to pick up routines almost instinctively, just as they will when herding sheep.

You can even devise an obstacle course for your pet at home. Start off with small jumps, and build up the height gradually. Ask the dog to stay, then go and stand at the opposite side of the jump and call your dog. Place a series of canes in the garden in a straight line, around 2.5 ft (0.75 m) apart, and encourage your pet to weave in and out through them. This will take time to learn, but your dog will be using up energy all the time and stay fit as a consequence.

Agility is actually quite a difficult skill for dogs to master, and even an experienced dog may forget to carry out all the stages in sequence, often missing one or two of the obstacles and then having to go back to them before proceeding farther down the course. You may be able to set up a routine with your dog by having particular hand signals to draw your pet around the poles. Most dogs will readily go through the tunnel.

Collies are particularly adept at agility training because of their good coordination skills.

These can be purchased from pet stores, or you can make one quite easily. Ultimately, you want to be in the situation where you can leave your dog at one end of the tunnel and call your pet through from the other end. During the initial training, it sometimes helps if you bend right down, with someone else holding your dog at the other end of the tunnel so that it can see your face. This is likely to encourage your pet to come through to you, and it will soon learn what is required.

Once proficient with these different elements, your dog will be well on the way to participating in an agility competition. However, you may find that your dog does badly in initial competitions, despite having performed well in practice. This is often a case of the dog being stage struck – being put off by the presence of an audience. This phase will soon pass, and your dog should start to grow in confidence and attain better results.

All dogs seem to enjoy agility tests, and it makes an exciting spectacle for viewers as well. Both training and participating in events will help to keep your pet fit and its weight in check. Dogs can take part in agility competitions well into middle age; it is not just an activity for younger dogs, who may be faster but are also likely to be wayward and acquire penalties for missing elements of the course.

Flyball

Another activity that is often seen at dog shows is a flyball competition. This is the ultimate team game for dogs, carried out on a relay basis. It tends to be smaller dogs that take part, including a relatively high proportion of Terriers and Collies. Teams, consisting of four dogs and their handlers, along with two reserves, compete against each other in what is a fast and highly enjoyable sport for participants and spectators alike. The dogs race over a series of four jumps down the course; these are calibrated according to the height of the smallest dog on each team, with 4in (10cm) being deducted from the height of the withers to determine the height of the jumps for each team.

The teams compete directly against each other in this sport, racing down well-spaced lanes that are 51ft (15.54m) long. This accommodates four jumps, spaced 10ft (3m) apart, with the fourth jump located 15ft (4.6m) from the flyball box, which effectively marks the halfway point in the course. Shaped like a large wedge, the flyball box has a spring-loaded front that releases a ball when the dog lands on it. All four dogs on each relay team have to retrieve the ball and then jump back over the hurdles to the finish line, before the next dog in that team can start the course. The winning team is the one that completes the course in the fastest time.

Teaching a dog to play flyball is a relatively slow process, because it is quite a complex sport and takes lots of time and training. There are also plenty of opportunities for things to go wrong.

These may include one of the contestants chasing a member of the opposite team instead of concentrating on the ball, missing a hurdle, failing to return with a ball or even setting off before the previous member of the team has returned across the start line.

Training consists of teaching your dog a series of different steps, so that it learns how to jump over all the hurdles, and then knows how to operate the box successfully, catch the ball and return back over the hurdles. Usually, the different sections are taught in reverse order, so that the sprint over the hurdles to the line forms the first part of the training process.

There are special classes where flyball is taught, but you can also teach these steps at home, reinforcing what you have learned in class. One of the most important aspects is calling your dog back to you, so that it returns at top speed, but without missing any of the hurdles. While many people enjoy taking part in flyball competitions for the fun of it, you can progress to serious competitions if your dog displays an aptitude for this sport.

Doggy Dancing

An unusual form of exercise for dogs that is becoming increasing popular is so-called doggy dancing, where a dog dances with its owner to music, although sometimes this is more prosaically billed as heelwork to music. Doggy dancing is a recent innovation in the dog world, only beginning in the 1990s. Displays of this type are often seen at the major dog shows, and inevitably arouse a lot of interest. With patience, there is no reason why you cannot teach some of these moves to your pet, and encourage this type of exercise at home, although you can actually hire professional doggy-dancing trainers.

Some breeds such as those of Bichon stock take naturally to doggy dancing. Incidentally, in the past they were often trained as circus performers.

Herding is a skill that comes naturally to some breeds, and there are even duck-herding competitions!

The more energetic steps should only be attempted with a fit dog that has no musculo-skeletal problems. At its most basic, doggy dancing entails setting basic training movements such as come, sit and stay to music; at its most extreme, the dog interacts with its owner in a much more athletic way, learning its cues in response to the music. Border Collies in particular appear to like standing up on their hindlegs and dancing with their owners, whereas other dogs frequently prefer to keep all four feet firmly on the ground.

Doggy dancing is something that owners confined to wheelchairs can do with their dogs, although it must be carried out indoors on a hard surface. The great thing is that, whatever your taste in music, you can develop a routine with your pet, who is likely to pick up on the excitement of the music and may, in some cases at least, respond to the beat.

Herding Clubs

In North America particularly, herding clubs have become popular for dogs whose working ancestry involved herding stock. This includes the various Sheepdogs and Shepherd Dogs, as well as Collies and similar breeds such as the Puli, originally from Hungary. Herding is essentially a working activity, so dogs must be fit before they will be accepted on to a programme of this type.

The training process is lengthy, because clearly dogs cannot be allowed to work with sheep unless adequately trained, to protect both the dog and the sheep from possible injury. However, it provides a great opportunity to see a different side to your dog, and one that will inevitably keep your pet fit, provided you maintain involvement in the programme. When you are out walking, it may be a good idea to avoid areas where you might come into contact with livestock, particularly sheep; if your dog starts to display herding instincts, this can create problems, especially at lambing time.

Cart Pulling and Sledding

Cart pulling is another way in which dogs can gain plenty of exercise by displaying their natural behaviour, and there are cart-pulling clubs in some areas. Various Mastiffs and Mountain Dogs, among others, have been used to pull carts, and entry to such clubs is normally restricted to those breeds that traditionally undertook this task. Not all breed members are accepted either, because they tend to be judged on temperament, with only friendly, co-operative dogs that will wear the necessary harness being chosen to participate.

The ability of dogs to provide transport has meant that they have sometimes also provided a vital life line to remote communities. A great example of this are the sled dogs that carried supplies of diphtheria serum to the Alaskan town of Nome back in 1925, when the town was otherwise cut off from the outside world, saving many lives as a result. This tradition is still maintained today, with a special race, known as the Iditarod Trail, taking place over the same route. This requires the highest levels of fitness, both from the dogs and those steering the sleds, who are called mushers.

In many areas today, less demanding sled-dog racing is a popular pursuit for breeds that benefit from plenty of activity. When there is snow on the ground, they can be used to pull sleds, but at other times of year they may be trained using wheeled carts, and are raced over set courses. Such is the energy expended in such activities that these dogs are likely to need additional calories, with special performance foods being marketed for them. This really is only an activity for those dogs that are completely fit, and have been bred for this purpose.

New Horizons

Once your dog has lost weight and is fit, you may find new opportunities open to you both. You may decide, for example, that you want to take your dog on a walking holiday, which in the past would not have been practical. As with other pursuits, this is something to work up to gradually by training in advance.

There are a number of hotels and guest houses that are willing to accept well-behaved dogs. Most dogs generally settle well without problems, particularly older individuals, but the key is to ensure that your dog gets sufficient exercise during the day so that it will settle down to sleep soundly in the evening when you go off to have a meal. Try to keep your pet awake during the day to encourage this. It helps if you pack some familiar items, such as your dog's bed. Remember also to take bedding, water bowls and a selection of your dog's favourite toys. It is also a good idea to take sufficient food for the trip, plus a towel and coat in case the weather turns bad.

You can plan your walking route quite easily in advance, and there are several guidebooks available that list suitable premises; local tourist boards should also be able to help, and you can do research on the internet. Dogs are very much at home on caravanning or camping trips, but again it is important to ensure that the sites accept dogs. This can be a much better option than booking your pet into kennels while you are away.

Fit for Life

Having slimmed down your pet, take care to ensure that you do not slip back into the old routines that gave rise to the problem in the first place. It can sometimes happen, particularly if you have concentrated largely on slimming your dog by dietary means, rather than by making changes in lifestyle. Keep monitoring your pet's weight, so that you can detect if the unwanted pounds start to creep back, and take action immediately to prevent the problem from becoming a crisis.

It will be worthwhile switching your dog to a senior diet as it gets older. This contains fewer calories and is more suited to the nutritional needs of older dogs. This change can take place typically around eight years old. If you are using fresh food for your pet, it may be advisable to cut back on the amount of food that you are offering in order to prevent unwanted weight gain.

Even though an older dog will not be as active as a youngster, and will instinctively not run as much, its quality of life will be significantly improved if it is in good condition and not overweight. This could easily add a year or more to your pet's lifespan.

If you take action to correct an obesity problem there is no reason your dog cannot go on to live a healthy, long and fulfilling life.

A Final Thought

Research is continuing into possible new ways of combating canine obesity in the future, with considerable emphasis now being placed on the development of safe, effective slimming pills. Yet whatever happens, the basic message will remain the same, in order to maximize your pet's long-term health and lifespan. Aim to prevent your pet becoming overweight in the first place, by a combination of sensible feeding and regular exercise.

As we have seen, there are many different activities which you can participate in with your dog to help him stay in shape, while not overlooking the benefits of going on regular walks each day as well. Even if you live in a relatively urban area, you will be able to increase your dog's level of fitness, and perhaps your own too, by participating in agility classes for example, which are often held in halls and similar venues. Taking part in events of this type is also likely to mean that both you and your pet will make new friends easily, in what is normally a very relaxed atmosphere.

SEARCHING FOR A MAGIC BULLET

There is as yet no simple way of slimming your dog down with tablets, but research is ongoing. Different approaches include the use of:

● A metabolite of a substance called DHEA which occurs naturally in the dog's body and has been shown to help to combat obesity.

● An extract from the white bean which has been recognized as a carbohydrate blocker, inhibiting its uptake from the dog's intestinal tract. This therefore results in the dog using its body fat to meet its energy requirements.

These types of treatment would still need to be used in combination with proper diet and exercise, for maximum effectiveness.

IDEAL WEIGHTS BY BREED

The figures here give a guide to the upper weight of the breed in each case. There may be some natural variance between different strains however, and also between dogs and bitches, but if your dog's weight is above the figure listed here, then almost certainly, he is too heavy. If you are in doubt, check with the chart on page 16.

Smallest breeds, measuring typically up to 12 in (30 cm)
Affenpinscher 9 lb (4.1 kg)
American Toy Terrier 6 lb (2.7 kg)
Australian Silky Terrier 10 lb (4.5 kg)
Australian Terrier 11 lb (5.0 kg)
Bichon Frise 12 lb (5.4 kg)
Bolognese 9 lb (4.1 kg)
Border Terrier 15.5 lb (7.0 kg)
Cairn Terrier 14 lb (6.4 kg)
Chihuahua 6 lb (2.7 kg)
Chinese Crested Dog 12 lb (5.4 kg)
Dandie Dinmont Terrier 18 lb (8.2 kg)
English Toy Terrier 8 lb (3.6 kg)
French Bulldog 28 lb (12.7 kg)
Griffon Bruxellois 11 lb (5.0 kg)
Havanese 12 lb (5.4 kg)
Japanese Chin 7 lb (3.2 kg)
King Charles Spaniel 14 lb (6.4 kg)
Lhasa Apso 15 lb (6.8 kg)
Lundehund 13 lb (5.9 kg)
Maltese 9 lb (4.1 kg)
Miniature Pinscher 10 lb (4.5 kg)
Norfolk Terrier 12 lb (5.4 kg)
Norwich Terrier 12 lb (5.4 kg)
Papillon 10 lb (4.5 kg)
Pekingese 12 lb (5.4 kg)
Pomeranian 5.5 lb (2.5 kg)
Poodle: Toy 15 lb (6.8 kg)
Pug 18 lb (8.2 kg)
Scottish Terrier 23 lb (10.4 kg)
Sealyham Terrier 20 lb (9.1 kg)
Shih Tzu 18 lb (8.2 kg)
Skye Terrier 25 lb (11.3 kg)
Tibetan Spaniel 15 lb (6.8 kg)
Welsh Corgi: Cardigan 29 lb (13.2 kg)
Welsh Corgi: Pembroke 24 lb (10.9 kg)
West Highland White Terrier 22 lb (10.0 kg)
Yorkshire Terrier 7 lb (3.2 kg)

Small breeds, measuring from 12-18 in (30-45 cm)
American Cocker Spaniel 28 lb (12.7 kg)
American Staffordshire Terrier 44 lb (20.0 kg)
Basenji 24 lb (10.9 kg)
Basset Artesian Normand 33 lb (15.0 kg)
Basset Fauve de Bretagne 44 lb (20.0 kg)
Basset Griffon Vendeen (Petit) 44 lb (20.0 kg)
Basset Hound 51 lb (23.1 kg)
Beagle 30lb (13.6 kg)
Bedlington Terrier 23 lb (10.4 kg)
Boston Terrier 25 lb (11.3 kg)
Bulldog 55 lb (25.0 kg)
Cavalier King Charles Spaniel 18 lb (8.2 kg)
Chow Chow 60lb (27.2 kg)
Clumber Spaniel 70 lb (31.8 kg)
Cocker Spaniel 32 lb (14.5 kg)
Eurasier 25 lb (11.3 kg)
Field Spaniel 50 lb (22.7 kg)
Finnish Spitz 36 lb (16.3 kg)
German Hunting Terrier 22 lb (10.0 kg)
German Spitz 40 lb (18.1 kg)
Glen of Imaal Terrier 35 lb (15.9 kg)
Irish Terrier 27 lb (12.2 kg)
Italian Greyhound 10 lb (4.5 kg)
Japanese Spitz 22 lb (10.0 kg)
Japanese Terrier 15 lb (6.8 kg)
Keeshond 66 lb (30.0 kg)
Lakeland Terrier 17 lb (7.7 kg)
Lowchen 11 lb (5.0 kg)
Luzerner Laufhund 44 lb (20.0 kg)
Manchester Terrier 18 lb (8.2 kg)
Norwegian Buhund 55 lb (25.0 kg)
Poodle: Miniature 26 lb (11.8 kg)
Poodle: Standard 49 lb (22.2 kg)
Schipperke 16 lb (7.2 kg)
Schnauzer: Miniature 15 lb (6.8 kg)
Schnauzer: Standard 33 lb (15.0 kg)
Shar-pei 55 lb (25.0 kg)
Shetland Sheepdog 18 lb (8.2 kg)
Smooth Fox Terrier 18 lb (8.2 kg)
Staffordshire Bull Terrier 38 lb (17.2 kg)
Sussex Spaniel 45 lb (20.4 kg)
Swedish Vallhund 31 lb (14.1 kg)
Tibetan Terrier 30 lb (13.6 kg)
Welsh Terrier 21 lb (9.5 kg)
Whippet 28 lb (12.7 kg)
Wire Fox Terrier 18 lb (8.2 kg)

IDEAL WEIGHTS BY BREED

Medium-sized breeds, measuring from 24-30 in (45-60 cm)

Airedale Terrier 44 lb (20.0 kg)
Australian Cattle Dog 66 lb (30.0 kg)
Bearded Collie 66 lb (30.0 kg)
Black Elkhound 44 lb (20.0 kg)
Border Collie 50 lb (22.7 kg)
Boxer 66 lb (30.0 kg)
Brittany 40 lb (18.1 kg)
Bull Terrier 62 lb (28.1 kg)
Dalmatian 55 lb (25.0 kg)
Elkhound 50 lb (22.7 kg)
English Springer Spaniel 50 lb (22.7 kg)
Flat-coated Retriever 70 lb (32 kg)
Golden Retriever 80 lb (36.2 kg)
Haldenstovare 55 lb (25.0 kg)
Hungarian vizsla 66 lb (30.0 kg)
Irish Setter 55lb (25.0kg)
Irish Water Spaniel 60 lb (27.2 kg)
Kerry Beagle 45 lb (20.4 kg)
Kerry Blue Terrier 37 lb (16.8 kg)
Labrador Retriever 75 lb (34.0 kg)
Munsterlander: large 65 lb (29.5 kg)
Munsterlander: small 33 lb (15.0 kg)
Nova Scotia Duck Tolling Retriever 65 lb (29.5 kg)
Old Danish Pointer 53 lb (24.0 kg)
Old English Sheepdog 66 lb (30.0 kg)
Portuguese Water Dog 40 lb (18.1 kg)
Rough Collie 65 lb (29.5 kg)
Siberian Husky 60 lb (27.2 kg)
Smooth Collie 45 lb (20.4 kg)
Welsh Springer Spaniel 45 lb (20.4 kg)
Wire-Haired Pointing Griffon 60 lb (27.2 kg)

Large breeds, measuring from 24-30 in (60-75 cm)

Afghan Hound 64 lb (29.0 kg)
Akita 88 lb (40.0 kg)
Alaskan Malamute 125 lb (56.7 kg)
Belgian Shepherd Dogs 62 lb (28.1 kg)
Berger Picard 75 lb (34.0 kg)
Bloodhound 110 lb (49.9 kg)
Borzoi 105 lb (47.6 kg)
Bouvier des Flandres 80 lb (36.3 kg)
Briard 75 lb (34.0 kg)
Bull Mastiff 130 lb (59.0 kg)
Chesapeake Bay Retriever 75 lb (34.0 kg)
Curly-coated Retriever 80 lb (36.3 kg)
Dobermann 80 lb (36.3 kg)
Dogue de Bordeaux 110 lb (49.9 kg)
English Setter 66 lb (30.0 kg)
German Long-haired Pointer 65 lb (29.5 kg)
German Rough-Haired Pointer 70 lb (31.7 kg)
German Shepherd dog 85 lb (38.6 kg)
German Short-haired Pointer 70 lb (31.8 kg)
Giant Schnauzer 77 lb (34.9 kg)
Gordon Setter 65 lb (29.5 kg)
Great Swiss Mountain dog 130 lb (60.0 kg)
Greyhound 70 lb (31.8 kg)
Hovawart 88 lb (40.0 kg)
Ibizan Hound 50 lb (22.7 kg)
Neapolitan Mastiff 155 lb (70.3 kg)
Newfoundland 150 lb (68 kg)
Otterhound 77 lb (35.0 kg)
Pharaoh Hound 65 lb (29.5 kg)
Picardy Spaniel 70 lb (31.8 kg)
Pointer 66 lb (30.0 kg)
Pyrenean Mountain Dog 110 lb (49.9 kg)
Rhodesian Ridgeback 85 lb (38.6 kg)
Rottweiler 110 lb (49.9 kg)
St. Bernard 121 lb (54.9 kg)
Saluki 66 lb (29.9 kg)
Spanish Pointer 66 lb (29.9 kg)
Swedish Elkhound 66 lb (29.9 kg)
Weimaraner 85 lb (38.6 kg)

Giant breeds over 30 in (75 cm) tall

Deerhound 105 lb (47.6 kg)
Great Dane 120 lb (54.4 kg)
Irish Wolfhound 120 lb (54.4 kg)
Leonberger 110 lb (49.9 kg)
Pyrenean Mastiff 155 lb (70.3 kg)

Index

accidents 92, 93
acupuncture 82
ages, relative 81
aggressiveness 48, 101, 116
agility competitions 132-4, 140
alcohol 112
amino acids 44
appetite 14, 41, 43, 45, 50, 87, 88, 102
arthritis 64, 76, 78-82
ascites 87
avocado 112

back problems 77, 78, 116
bacteria 43, 48, 67, 100, 102
balls see toys & balls
bathing dogs 70, 130, 131
beaches 69-71
begging 37, 72, 94, 95, 99
behaviour problems see specific problems
(eg aggressiveness)
bird food 109
bloat 31
blood sugar levels 43, 50, 82, 83, 84, 85
body temperature 38, 45, 54, 61-2, 87, 105,
107
bones 118
boredom & mental stimulation 28, 37, 60,
61, 97, 106, 116, 119, 121
brachycephalic (short-faced) dogs 58, 61,
114
bread dough 112
breeds 12-13, 18-21, 38
    breed standards 16, 19-20, 108, 141
    breed-specific diets 22, 47, 54
    exercise requirements 57-9, 105, 139
    obesity risks 14, 21, 34, 35, 44
    see also specific groups (eg hounds) & size
    groups (eg large breeds)
bribery 40, 89

calories
    energy requirements 14, 37, 41, 45, 50,
    54-6, 107, 138
    in dry food 46
    in home-made foods 43, 48, 98, 107-8
    in treats 24, 40
    in wet food 46
cani-cross racing 128-9
canine cognitive dysfunction 119
canine gravy mix 46
canine teeth 42, 71
canned foods 22, 33, 35, 37, 107
carbohydrates 43, 48, 49, 51, 56, 84, 98
carnassial teeth 42, 43
cars 80, 114
cart pulling 137-8
castration see neutering
cataracts 85
cats & cat food 44, 68, 111
causes of obesity 9, 14, 21, 27-8, 31, 35, 38,
60, 74
    health problems 85-8, 92, 93

overfeeding 22, 25, 28, 41, 54-6, 95
Celebratory Cereal Crunch recipe 56
cellulose 48, 50
cereals see carbohydrates; fibre
chews 100, 116-17
chiggers 68
children 22, 103, 109
chocolate 110
chrondroprotectants 81
clicker training 39
coats (garments) 61-2, 79
coats (hair) 61, 64, 105, 130
collars see leashes & collars
complementary treatments 82
congestive heart failure 91-2
constipation 50, 101
coprophagia 102
crocodilians 65
cross-breeds 16, 18, 39
Cruft, Charles 20, 21
Cushing's disease 87
cycling 125-7

dangers & safety
    accidents 92, 93
    cars 114
    exercise 61, 65-71, 105, 114, 116, 125,
    126-7
    foods 110-12
destructive behaviour 97, 116
diabetes 50, 53, 54, 82-5
diaries 15, 108
diarrhoea 54, 100, 112
diet see foods
dietary fibre 44, 48, 50, 84, 98
digestion & digestive problems 43, 50,
100-2
dog-napping 114
dog parks & gyms 123
dog shows 19-21
dog-walking & sitting services 30, 104
doggy dancing 135-6
domestication 8, 10, 19-20, 57
dough 112
dry foods 22, 33, 35, 37, 43, 46, 48, 49, 107

eating disorders 102
energy requirements 14, 37, 41, 45, 50,
54-6, 107, 138
essential amino acids 44
essential fatty acids 51-2
exercise
    amounts required 26, 28, 57-9, 105, 113-
    19, 139, 140
    dangers & safety 61, 65-71, 105, 114, 116,
    125, 126-7
    dog-walking & sitting services 30, 104
    health checks 125
    off-leash 59, 60, 119, 123
    older dogs 27, 58, 61, 62, 64, 127, 130,
    139
    osteoarthritis 64, 79-80

toys & balls 59, 62-4, 65, 71, 114-19
two dogs 59, 121, 123
weather 61-2, 71, 79, 105, 113, 127, 129
when & where 31, 61-2, 66, 96-7, 113, 140
see also specific types (eg swimming) &
locations (eg beaches)
exocrine pancreatic insufficiency 47, 54

false pregnancies 88, 116
'fancying' 19
farmstock 69, 126
fat cells 38, 51, 82
fats 49, 51-4, 109
fatty acids 51-2, 81
feeding
    feeding routines 37, 95-6, 101, 106, 123
    overfeeding 22, 25, 28, 41, 54-6, 95
fibre 44, 48, 50, 84, 98
fitness 11, 26, 138-9
flatulence 47, 50, 98
fleas 67-8, 123
fluid build-up 87
flyball 134-5
flying discs 63-4, 118-19
foods
    bland meals 100
    food industry 21-2, 47
    food toys 119
    harmful 110-12
    labels 49, 107
    measuring 22, 24, 101, 103
    nutritional content 22, 45, 47-8, 49, 50,
    51-2, 81
    preferences & palatability 32-5, 46, 47-8
    quantity guidelines 54-6
    storage & use-by dates 52
    texture 35
    variety 33, 36, 37
    warm foods 46, 48
    see also specific diets (eg vegetarian
diets); specific nutrients (eg
carbohydrates); specific types (eg canned
foods); treats
frozen foods 33
fussy eaters 35, 36, 37, 46

giant breeds 31, 58, 73, 107, 141
glucose 43, 50, 82, 84
gluten-free diets 47
grapes 112
grassjoring 129
gravy mix 46
grey wolf see wolves
gundogs 12, 18, 125, 139

harvest mites 68
health problems see specific problems (eg
diabetes)
heart conditions 61, 91-2, 127
heat (bitches) 74, 82, 110
heat stroke 61, 69, 105, 109, 114
heelwork to music 135-6

herding clubs 136
herding dogs 13, 18, 69, 97, 136
hide & seek 119
high-fibre foods 44, 48, 50, 84, 98
hiking 125
hip dysplasia 75, 79, 125
holidays 138
home-made foods 33, 43, 47-8, 52, 98, 107-8, 139
hookworm 68-9
hormonal problems 82-8
hotels 138
hounds 10, 12, 14, 18, 57, 121, 125, 139
humans see owners
hydrotherapy 64, 80, 130
hypoallergenic diets 47
hypothyroidism 85-7

illness see specific problems (eg diabetes)
inedible objects, swallowing 71, 100, 102
infections 48, 67, 74, 85, 88, 123
injuries 92, 93
insulin 82, 84, 85
insurance 127
intestinal blockages 100-1

jogging 127
joint problems & arthritis 64, 75, 76, 77, 78-82, 125
joint-protector substances 81

large breeds 14, 31, 45, 73, 75, 81, 107, 141
leashes & collars 71, 99, 122, 126, 128-9
lifestage diets 22, 45, 47
ligaments, torn 75-6
linoleic acid 52
lite (weight-loss) foods 47, 48, 50, 52, 98, 107
livestock 69, 126
Lyme disease 67

macadamia nuts 110
mammary tumours 73, 74
meat 32, 44, 48, 118
medium breeds 81, 133, 141
mental stimulation see boredom & mental stimulation
minerals 48, 98
mites, harvest 68
mongrels 16, 18, 39
monitoring dog's weight 9, 15, 39, 72, 107, 108, 138
mountain biking 125-7
mouth, opening dog's 115
multi-pet households 111, 120-3
    see also cats

neutering 27, 73-4, 83, 88

obedience training see training
obesity
    breeds at risk 14, 21, 34, 35, 44
    controlling see specific methods (eg exercise)

owners' obesity 9, 21, 25, 26
    reasons for see causes of obesity
    recognising 16-18, 89
    slimming pills research 140
off-leash exercise 59, 60, 119, 123
    see also specific types (eg jogging)
older dogs 81
    exercise 58, 61, 62, 64, 119, 127, 130, 139
    food 27, 45, 50, 54, 56, 81, 139
osteoarthritis 64, 76, 78-82
overfeeding 22, 25, 28, 41, 54-6, 95
overweight, definition 16
    see also obesity
owners
    children 22, 103, 109
    lifestyle changes 28
    obesity problems 9, 21, 25, 26
    owner/dog fitness programmes 26
    owner/dog relationships 25, 28, 89-90, 94-7, 106

pancreatic insufficiency 47, 54
pancreatitis 53-4
parasites 67-9, 123
pastoral dogs 12, 18, 69, 97, 136, 139
people see owners
pet gyms 123
pica 102
plaque 43
possessiveness 88, 101, 116, 117
pregnancies 90-1, 110
    false 88, 116
prescription diets 47, 56, 85, 98
probiotics 100
protein 44, 49, 56
puppies 33-5, 38-9, 45, 58, 72-3, 90-1, 115, 123
pyometra 74, 88

radio 121
raisins 112
ramps 80
running & jogging 127-9

safety see dangers & safety
scavenging & stealing 11, 28, 71, 99, 100, 102, 103, 108-12
scenthounds 12, 14, 18, 125, 139
scraps 25, 37, 54, 72, 103, 108
semi-moist foods 22, 33, 35, 84
senior dogs see older dogs
senses 10, 41, 131
sheep-worrying 69, 136
sighthounds 10, 12, 14, 18, 57, 121, 125, 139
skijoring 129
skin cancer 105
sled dogs 47, 51, 52, 127, 128, 129, 138-9
sledding 137-8
slimming pills, research 140
slipped discs 77, 78, 116
small breeds 33, 35, 45, 53, 73, 81, 107, 110, 126-7, 132, 141
    see also toy dogs
smell, sense of 41, 131

snakes & snake bites 66-7
spaying see neutering
specialist diets 47
spitz breeds 12, 129
Spratt, James 21
stealing see scavenging & stealing
straying 110
swimming 64-5, 71, 80, 130

table scraps 25, 37, 54, 72, 103, 108
target weights 16, 39, 107, 108, 141
teeth & dental problems 42-3, 45, 71
television 121
terriers 12-13, 18, 54, 139
tethering dogs 105
thryoid problems 85-7
ticks 67
tidbits see treats
torn ligaments 75-6
toy dogs 13, 18, 21, 46, 59, 102, 107, 127, 139
    see also small breeds
toys & balls 59, 62-4, 65, 71, 114-19
training
    basic obedience 60, 61, 69, 97, 123, 126-7
    toys and play 63, 115, 117, 119
    treats & alternatives 39-40, 72-3
treats 24-5, 28, 72-3, 89-90, 95-6, 97, 107, 109
    alternatives to 24, 39-40, 96, 103, 106
    bones 118
    Celebratory Cereal Crunch recipe 56
    see also scraps
tug toys 116, 117
turnspit 8

utility dogs 12, 18, 137-8, 139

vegetables 98
vegetarian diets 33, 44, 47
vitamins 48, 98, 102
volvulus 31
vomiting 53, 100, 110, 112

walks see exercise
weather 61-2, 71, 79, 105, 113, 127, 129
weighing dogs 15, 108
weight control
    benefits 28
    maintenance 107, 124, 138-9, 140
    monitoring 9, 15, 39, 72, 107, 108, 138
    target weights 16, 39, 107, 108, 141
weight-loss clinics 92-3
weight-loss (lite) foods 47, 48, 50, 52, 98, 107
weight-loss schedules 108
wet foods 22, 33, 35, 43, 46, 49
wolves 10, 11, 37, 41, 44, 49, 57, 60, 102
working dogs 8, 10, 12-13, 14, 19-21, 47, 69, 97
    see also specific groups (eg hounds)
worms 68-9

With many thanks to everyone at Cassell Illustrated who contributed to this project, particularly Joanne Wilson, not forgetting Tony Cohen and Michelle Pickering.

I am very also grateful to my daughter Lucinda for her assistance, and James and Mandy at Watson, Little Ltd., as well as Lucy the Basset Hound for inspiration!